THE PERFORMANCE OF
ITALIAN BASSO CONTINUO

For Frances and Mario

The Performance of
Italian Basso Continuo
Style in Keyboard Accompaniment in the
Seventeenth and Eighteenth Centuries

GIULIA NUTI

ASHGATE

Published by
Ashgate Publishing Limited
Gower House
Croft Road
Aldershot
Hants GU11 3HR
England

Ashgate Publishing Company
Suite 420
101 Cherry Street
Burlington, VT 05401-4405
USA

Ashgate website: http://www.ashgate.com

British Library Cataloguing in Publication Data
Nuti, Giulia
  The performance of Italian basso continuo: style in
  keyboard accompaniment in the seventeenth and eighteenth centuries
  1. Continuo – Italy – History – 17th century 2. Continuo –
  Italy – History – 18th century
  I. Title
  781.4'7

Library of Congress Cataloging-in-Publication Data
Nuti, Giulia, 1976-
  The performance of Italian basso continuo: style in keyboard accompaniment in the
seventeenth and eighteenth centuries / by Giulia Nuti.
      p. cm.
  Includes bibliographical references.
  ISBN-13: 978-0-7546-0567-6 (alk. paper)
  ISBN-10: 0-7546-0567-1 (alk. paper)
  1. Continuo–Italy. 2. Performance practice (Music) 3. Music–Italy–History and
criticism. I. Title.
  ML442.N87 2006
  781.47–dc22

                                                                            2006021141

ISBN 978-0-7546-0567-6

Printed and bound in Great Britain by TJ International Ltd, Padstow, Cornwall.

Contents

List of Music Examples

Preface

This book is a study of the performance of basso continuo accompaniment in Italian music from the late 1500s to the end of the eighteenth century. It offers a performance-derived answer to the problems posed by music with few, and sometimes no, indications on how to play from notations that apparently leave so much to the discretion of the performer. The book draws upon primary sources to elicit an account of performance practices as they developed and transformed over the period. As well as a careful consideration of contemporary treatises, aspects of performance were gleaned from indications and specific instructions, or rules, and inferences in contemporary documents, which are extensively quoted in support of the interpretative arguments. Much of this material is extant only in manuscript sources that have never been published; some of it survives in rare printed editions of the time; a few sources are available in facsimile or modern editions. The study and performance of the music of the period, both solo and in ensemble, is a most important indicator of the applicability of many of the written texts. Modern scholars have been consulted although my approach has been to make particular use of primary sources; stylistic practice in basso continuo accompaniment is sometimes drawn from treatises from other times and other musical cultures, and neither consults nor reflects two and a half centuries of diverse and wonderful Italian music.

Italian basso continuo accompaniment displays a coherent development that requires the performer to play in keeping with where in that development a musical work lies; there is no single practice that meets the time span of musical creation from the late 1500s to the late 1700s; consequently musical practices are presented here chronologically, informing appropriate performance as it altered over the decades.

The effect in performance of the stylistic guides that have reached us required a familiarity with original Italian instruments, what they sounded like, and what possibilities they allowed; their study ran parallel to the research on the written texts.

The English versions of the Italian quotations are as accurate a rendition as possible of the Italian text, rather than an English paraphrase, even where this yields unwieldly English constructions, to allow direct comparison with the original text; it has not been possible always to maintain original, early Italian punctuation in the translations but abbreviations and contractions in the Italian text have been given at length, as is the practice in the reprinting of early Italian.

Apart from undisputed instrument names – harpsichord, organ, lute, violin – all other names of instruments have been left in the original Italian in the translations, so that the instrument is named unambiguously. Markings and usages in text and musical instructions have sometimes been left in Italian where this is preferable to an only approximate English term and there is familiarity with Italian usage (for example *acciaccatura*). Plurals of Italian words are as in Italian.

Musical examples have been recopied where this aids the presentation of the argument. In such cases, the soprano (C 1) clef has been changed to the treble (G 2) clef, accidentals have been modernized and, where appropriate, two staves have been used instead of three; in all other respects the notation of the original has been retained (for example, key signatures, time signatures, beams). Editorial amplifications of figuring are marked in square brackets.

Nigel Farrow first suggested that I should write a study of accompaniment of Italian song; Rachel Lynch encouraged this larger project on Italian accompaniment. As College Musician of Queens' College Cambridge I was made most welcome by the President and the Fellowship; their support provided the opportunity to work on much of this book.

Giulia Nuti
Florence, December 2006

Acknowledgements

In writing this book I received generous support from King's College Cambridge for research in Bologna and the Churchill Memorial Foundation for research in the libraries and private collections in Venice, Florence, Rome and Naples.

The librarians and staff of libraries in Italy were especially kind. I am most grateful to the Civico Museo Bibliografico Musicale in Bologna, where Oscar Mischiati had various discussions with me on Italian music, and guided me through the anonymous treatises held in the library; the Biblioteca Nazionale Centrale, Florence (Sala Musica and Sala Manoscritti e Rari), the Biblioteca Berenson Villa I Tatti, Florence; the Biblioteca del Conservatorio San Pietro a Majella, Naples. The Bibliothèque du Conservatoire Royal de Bruxelles and the Bibliothèque Nationale de France, Paris were most helpful. The librarians and staff of the British Library, the Royal College of Music Library, the Pendlebury Library of the Faculty of Music, University of Cambridge, the Rowe Music Library, King's College and the University Library, Cambridge were of the greatest assistance, and to them all I am indebted.

I thank the owners and curators of the instruments in the Museo degli Strumenti Musicali, Castello Sforzesco, Milan; Musée des Instruments de Musique, Brussels; the Cobbe Collection of Keyboard Instruments, Hatchlands; the Early Keyboard Instrument Collection, Fenton House; the Royal College of Music Museum of Instruments, and many other private collections in Italy, Belgium, France, Germany and Britain for allowing me to play historic Italian instruments in their care. My thanks to Augusto Bonza for teaching me so much about how harpsichords, particularly Italian harpsichords, are built and work.

Luigi Ferdinando Tagliavini was kind enough to allow me to play the beautiful harpsichords in his collection of instruments in Bologna, and to discuss with me various topics touched upon here; I was honoured to receive his comments on an earlier draft of the text.

Gerald Gifford's encouragement and detailed remarks and suggestions on the text were most generous. Flora Dennis commented closely on the sixteenth-century material; Andrew Lawrence-King discussed the seventeeth century extensively with me; Frédérick Haas offered insight on harpsichord performance techniques. Milena Nuti helped me order large amounts of argument and Frances Welch worked with me on various drafts of the book. I am most grateful to Andrew Jones, who commented extensively on a previous version of the text.

Federico Maria Sardelli, Bettina Hoffmann and Gian Luca Lastraioli contributed their performance skills and musicological knowledge; Nicki Kennedy, Sally Bruce-Payne, André Henrich and Arno Peck played and sang with me during these years of research; Valerio Losito gave me insight into the accompaniment of solo instruments and played much of the seventeenth-century reperoire with me; we all tried out the techniques described here. My pupils at the Scuola di Musica di Fiesole raised many of the queries to which I have sought the answers.

I am most grateful to Andrea Paoletti and Monica Fintoni who drafted translations of the numerous quotations; all musical examples were transcribed by Nicola Mitolo using the Wedelmusic programme. To him and the Assocazione Musica Attiva (www.musicaattiva.it) are due my warmest thanks.

I thank Frances and Domenico Mario Nuti for their constant assistance and advice. Enrico Amante gave unfailing support and encouragement in all the travelling, research, performing and writing, made so many musicians welcome in Florence and listened to so many hours of music; to him more than anyone, thank you.

List of Abbreviations

BBc	Brussels, Bibliothèque du Conservatoire Royal de Musique
GBLbl	London, The British Library
IBc	Bologna, Museo internazionale e biblioteca della musica di Bologna
IFn	Florence, Biblioteca Nazionale Centrale
IMc	Milan, Biblioteca del Conservatorio 'Giuseppe Verdi'
IMOe	Modena, Biblioteca Estense Universitaria
INc	Naples, Biblioteca del Conservatorio di Musica S. Pietro a Majella
IRli	Rome, Biblioteca dell'Accademia Nazionale dei Lincei e Corsiniana
IRn	Rome, Biblioteca Nazionale Centrale 'Vittorio Emanuele II'
IRvat	Rome, Biblioteca Apostolica Vaticana
IVnm	Venice, Biblioteca Nazionale Marciana

Chapter 1

Introduction

Basso continuo performance, its teaching, and practice informs and reflects the wealth of musical styles that characterize Italian music from the end of the sixteenth century to the last decades of the eighteenth century. In this book rare and less accessible sources are considered, as well as some of the most famous and well-known texts, bringing the playing of basso continuo in the Italian style into a focus that displays it in all its complexity and diversity. Rules and instructions in the published books and treatises are considered alongside the manuscript sources on basso continuo and, most importantly, emphasis is placed on the music itself in order to interpret and illuminate the printed treatises.

Beginning with a consideration of various forms of accompaniment in use in the most musically influential Italian cities in the sixteenth century, it will be seen how and why basso continuo came to be the most widely adopted system of accompaniment until the beginning of the Classical period.

Indications and clues on the performance of seventeenth-century music must be sought in the introductions to the first operas and songbooks, in the early treatises, in accounts of musical performances, and through comparisons of practices used in the solo repertoire. Issues of instrumentation are also addressed and systems of notation applicable to lutes, guitars and theorboes are touched upon for their implication in the execution of the accompaniment.

Later, in the 1700s, practical exercises that rehearse the skills needed for basso continuo performance on keyboard instruments in particular begin to appear. These are considered alongside indications for continuo playing found in scores; the solo repertoire of the period is drawn upon also.

Basso continuo brought an innovative feature to performance: the capacity to respond to each and every interpretation of a work through improvisation. This system of accompaniment was developed specifically for lutes, theorboes, harps, harpsichords and organs, to name the most commonly used; its influence corresponds exactly to the historical period in which these instruments were in vogue. So perfectly did it respond to their capacities and limitations that, once established, it displaced any other means of notation for the accompaniment of any work, from solo to orchestral. It allowed dynamics and expressiveness on keyboard instruments: accompanists could choose whether to play *tasto solo*, or large loud chords, and could adapt their realization of the accompaniment according to what was being sung.[1]

---

[1]   There is further and more detailed discussion of the reasons for the introduction of basso continuo at the beginning of Chapter 3.

As early as 1568, Vincenzo Galilei wrote:

Ma se noi volessimo per il contrario discorrere l'imperfettione, e mancamenti de sopraddetti strumenti, e particularmente quelle del meno imperfetto, che è l'Organo; ... non per diffetto del'Arte e saper loro ma della natura dello strumento, [gli organisti] non hanno possuto, non possano, ne potranno mai, esprimere gli effetti delle Armonie come la durezza, mollezza, asprezza, e dolcezza; e consequentemente i gridi, i lamenti, gli stridi, i pianti, e ultimamente la quiete e 'l furore, con tanta grazia, e maraviglia, come gli Eccellenti Sonatori nel Liuto fanno, e forse che queste non sono annoverate tra le principali cagioni le quali la Musica è sempre stata ed è in pregio.[2]

[But if we want to talk about the defects and deficiencies of the aformentioned instruments and, particularly those of the least imperfect, which is the organ, ... not for lack of their Art or knowledge but because of the nature of the instrument [organists] have been unable, cannot, could never, express the effects of the harmonies such as the harshness, melodiousness, tartness and sweetness; and, subsequently, the yells, the wails, the shrieks, the laments and, lastly, the calm and the fury, with such charm and wonder as do the first-rate lute players; and are these not counted among the main reasons why Music is and always has been held in high esteem.]

Already he was recognizing that while lutes were able to accompany with more sensitivity and dynamics than keyboard instruments, more was required of both; the written out *intavolature* of the time did not allow the accompanist to respond to the 'calm and the fury' for the very reason that these *were* written out.

Writing about Improvisation

Writings on basso continuo illustrate with what difficulty practice in music was diffused. Very few of the early printed treatises speak of how to realize basso continuo in a practical situation, tending instead to concentrate on describing harmonic principles. Performance skills were taught aurally; those instructions that have reached us have done so in great part through contemporary documents and letters, manuscripts, the introductions to music books and, only much later, in the systematization of information embodied in the printed treatises of the eighteenth century.

Contemporary Written-out Accompaniments

There are three types of contemporary written-out accompaniments – none of these can be taken as a thorough and complete testimony to basso continuo realization in any style because it is, by definition, impossible to fully notate

---

[2]   Vincenzo Galilei, *Fronimo dialogo di Vincenzo Galilei fiorentino* (Venice, 1568), p. 51.

an improvisation. The first type is made up of the most simple, harmonic accompaniments to the songs of the early 1600s; however, these are out of keeping with the style of accompaniment described and taught at the time (discussed on pp. 33–4). The second consists of harmonic realizations of the early 1700s; these are an attempt to annotate the complex harmonies and ornamentation intrinsic to performance and confirm in music many of the rules explained in the treatises of the time. Unfortunately, none is written by a master; rather, they are produced by minor composers and unknown authors keen on demonstrating every variation of the rules, producing realizations that overemphasize extravagance and break the first rule of accompaniment – the exercise of judgement and good taste (pp. 92–4). The third type of composed accompaniment is intended as an integral part of a work in the form of an accompaniment – the function of this type is wholly different from that of a basso continuo accompaniment (pp. 79–81). While accompaniments of this last type certainly are indicative of the view of one person at one time, there is no spontaneity of elaboration or response to whatever is being accompanied.

The information to be gained from treatises is mostly theoretical and must be evaluated, indeed can only be evaluated, in conjunction with musical sources. It is vital to emphasize the importance of the musical sources themselves as they provide the most secure performance guidance in showing what composers implicitly required, or even sometimes instructed a performer to do, rather than consisting of advice from musicians who were not necessarily composers or performers but theoreticians who may not have wished to reveal all the information needed to understand or evaluate their statements.

'Professional secrets' are another reason, and an important one, why so many printed treatises are inadequately descriptive of performance; this applies to all treatises of the seventeenth century. Zacconi, writing of Costanzo Porta addressing his students, notes this attitude: 'Per mille Ducati, io non haverei dato fuori i secreti ch'à dato questo frate' ['Not for a thousand ducats would I [Porta] have revealed the secrets given away by this friar [Zacconi]'].[3]

While some of the most valuable instruction is often illustrated in the music itself, the intrinsically improvisatory nature of basso continuo provides a further reason why this is such a difficult subject to explain in words alone, as Alessandro Scarlatti confirms in a manuscript source, advising the scholar to consult him directly:

Altre circostanze accidentali richieste dall'armonia dello stile di questo presente scrittore da lui trovate nel più nobil modo di sonare, non ponno darsi in scritto, mà à voce, colle varie maniere de' movimenti della mano nel sonare; al che si riserba.[4]

[Other accidentals dictated by the harmony of the style of the present writer, which he has found to be in the most beautiful manner of playing, cannot be given in writing,

---

3   Ludovico Zacconi, *Prattica di musica* (Venice, 1596), vol. 2, p. 5.
4   Alessandro Scarlatti (GBLbl, MS Add. 14244), p. 40.

but only verbally, with the various ways of moving the hand when playing, which he finds indispensable.]

For the same reason not only performance, but composition too, is poorly represented in the writings of the time. At the beginning of the 1600s the new style of composition, the *genere rappresentativo*, is established; however, typically of the period, there is no contemporary text on composition that explains how to write in the new genre. Monteverdi wished to remedy the lack of texts on how to compose in *genere rappresentativo*; having found himself without a guide he hoped to write a guide for others:

> Vado credendo che non sarà discaro al mondo, posciachè ho provato in pratica che quando fui per scrivere il pianto del Arianna, non trovando libro che mi aprisse la via naturale alla immaginatione nè meno che mi illuminasse che dovessi essere immitatore, altri che platone per via di un suo lume rinchiuso così che appena potevo di lontano con la mia debil vista quel poco che mi mostrava; ho provato dico la gran fatica che mi bisognò fare in far quel poco ch'io feci d'immitatione, et perciò spero sij per non dispiacere ma rieschi come si voglia che alla fine son per contentarmi d'essere più tosto poco lodato nel novo, che molto nel ordinario scrivere.[5]

> [I believe that it will not be displeasing to the world, for I found in practice that when I was about to compose the Lament of Arianna – finding no book that could guide my imagination intuitively, nor one that would enlighten me as to whom I ought to be imitating (other than [as in] Plato, [but with] a light so hidden that I could hardly discern from afar with my feeble sight what little he showed me) – I found, I was saying, what hard work I had to do in order to achieve the little I did do through imitation, and I therefore hope it is not going to be displeasing, whatever the result may be, as in the end I would sooner be praised for innovation in the new style than greatly praised for the re-presentation of the known.]

His book *Melodia, overo seconda pratica musicale* was never written.

It is as hard today as it was then to write a book about the nature of the improvisation that is basso continuo, and it is to be expected that it should be hard; Italian composers relied on the thorough professionalism, technical competence and good taste of their musicians when explaining how their music should be performed, or when writing of style, and did not intend or hope to communicate all in words alone.

---

[5]   Claudio Monteverdi, *Lettere*, from Venice, 22 October 1633, ed. Domenico De' Paoli (Rome, 1973).

Chapter 2

Forms of Accompaniment in the Sixteenth Century

In order to understand how and why basso continuo came about and account for the stylistic interpretation of basso continuo from 1600 onwards, it is helpful to undertake a study of accompanying instruments, the music they were playing, and their function within the ensemble during the 1500s.

Stylistic turning points in accompaniment coincide with changes in musical composition. The most important and fundamental change in compositional style that ran through the 1500s was the shift in importance from multi-voiced polyphonic works to more harmonically conceived pieces. Despite counterpoint being the strongest, most prominent compositional technique of the time, harmony was present and played an important part in accompaniments.

Multi-voiced polyphony was the most frequently used compositional style of the period; if voices were missing in performance these were filled in by an accompanying instrument, a *strumento perfetto*, so called because of a capacity to play harmonies as well as counterpoint, such as the lute, harpsichord, organ, viol or *lira*. Yet what had begun as a way of making up for missing voices began to be welcomed as a genre in itself. As early as 1528 Castiglione describes the accompaniment of a voice by a lute, consort of viols, or keyboard as one of the most refined and desirable ways of making music, as a respite from so many voices singing confusedly and mixing up words:

Allor il Signor Gaspar Pallavicino 'Molte sorti di musica,' disse, 'si trovano, così di voci vive, come di istrumenti; però a me piacerebbe intendere qual sia la migliore tra tutte et a che tempo debba il cortegiano operarla.' 'Bella musica,' rispose messer Federico 'parmi il cantar bene a libro sicuramente e con bella maniera, ma ancor molto più il cantare alla viola perchè tutta la dolcezza consiste quasi in un solo, e con molto maggior attenzion si nota e si intende il bel modo e l'aria non essendo occupate le orecchie in più che una sola voce, e meglio ancora vi si discerne ogni piccolo errore; il che non accade cantando in compagnia perchè l'uno aiuta l'altro. Ma sopra tutto parmi gratissimo il cantare alla viola per recitare; il che tanto di venustà ed efficacia aggiunge alle parole, che è gran maraviglia. Sono ancora armoniosi tutti gli istrumenti da tasti, perché hanno le consonanze molto perfette e con facilità vi si possono far molte cose che empiono l'animo di musicale dolcezza. E non meno diletta la musica delle quattro viole da arco, la quale è soavissima et artificiosa. Dà ornamento e grazia assai la voce umana a tutti questi instrumenti, de' quali voglio che al nostro cortegian basti aver notizia; e quanto più però in essi sarà eccellente, tanto sarà meglio.'[1]

[Then Signor Gaspar Pallavicino remarked: 'Many different kinds of music exist, both vocal and instrumental. So I would like to understand which is the best of all and on which occasion the courtier should use it.' 'Beautiful music,' answered Federico, 'consists, in my opinion, in fine singing *a libro*, with a lovely manner, and even more in singing to the accompaniment of the lute because all the sweetness is contained in a solo [voice], and with greater attention one notes and hears the fine manner and style as the ears are not occupied by more than one voice, and every little fault, too, is more clearly apparent; this does not happen with more people as one [singer] helps the other. But above all, it seems to me most pleasant to sing accompanied by the lute; it adds so much beauty and effectiveness to the words, as to make one marvel. All fretted and keyboard instruments, indeed, are full of harmony, because their consonances are perfect and, with ease, it is possible to do many things that fill the soul with musical sweetness. And no less delightful is the playing of four viols, which is most suave and artful. The human voice adds ornament and grace to all these instruments, about which I believe enough has been said for our courtier; the more he may excel in these, the better.'][2]

His choice of lutes, viols and keyboards, the courtier's accompanying instruments, suggests he is describing the accompaniment of a madrigal, rather than a popular song belonging to a more aural tradition, where accompaniment was still played by a harmonic instrument such as a guitar. In the instance Castiglione is describing the accompanist would have intabulated the multi-voiced madrigals and played all the parts on keyboard instruments or lutes.

Simplifying Counterpoint

To play more than three or four voices contrapuntally on anything other than a keyboard is possible only up to a certain point and very difficult; it was a skill that rendered the music accessible only to the accomplished lutenist who, through training, was able to play all the counterpoint directly off the parts, or would intabulate the parts for personal use; this may be the reason why so few publications, and even fewer manuscript examples, survive. It became desirable to open up the genre to a wider public of less experienced players; publications began to appear where the soprano voice is accompanied by just two voices (tenor and bass), rather than an intabulation of all the voices.

---

[1]   Baldassarre Castiglione, *Il libro del Cortegiano* (Florence, 1528), book II, chapter XIII.

[2]   The Italian *viola* was translated in the English contemporary text as a lute. In Italian, at this time, *viola* was synonymous with lute; indeed Castiglione specifies *viole da arco* to mean viols.

In 1509–11 Petrucci published Franciscus Bossinensis's transcriptions of *frottole*,[3] mainly by Cara and Tromboncino, arranged and simplified for the lute. In a letter of 1515, Pero Soranzo wrote to Mario Contarini describing a dinner held at the Gonzaga's: 'Poi si andò a cena benissimo preparato, e poi ce ne vene in uno camerino Marcheto e un altro con do làuti, che disse certe canzone che mai si sentì meglio' ['Then we went to very well-prepared dinner, and then, in a little chamber, Marcheto and another, with two lutes, performed some songs that were never heard better'].[4] The Marcheto referred to was the celebrated Marchetto Cara, whose works were intabulated by Bossinensis. That so early, in 1515, voices should be singing just to lutes confirms that singing a single vocal line to the accompaniment of an instrument was regarded as a highly desirable combination.[5] In 1536 Willaert intabulated Verdelot's madrigals; this publication is more important than that of Bossinensis, for the lute part is more complex.[6]

Even though the first printed books with this type of accompaniment date from the first decade of the 1500s, it should be remembered that the tradition of accompanying pieces in such a manner must have reached even further back. As the function of the lute in the accompaniment of polyphonic pieces was exactly that of filling in missing voices, it is no surprise that publications start to appear where well-known songs are reduced to one voice and simple accompaniment, confirmation in print that this was an already established tradition.

These accompaniments play an important role in the gradual shift in ascendancy from counterpoint to harmony and they illustrate it well: in these arrangements, what were five-part madrigals with separate voices and voice-leading are reduced to harmonic blocks accompanying the soprano line. The complexity of multi-voiced pieces, in which words were sacrificed for the melodic line, no longer satisfied, and changes came about in the style of composition; while, in the vocal madrigals, the main compositional interest had concentrated on the relationship between the voices, and each vocal part was of equal importance, now the entire interest of the piece lay in the single melodic line, accompanied by an instrument. Accompaniments had not been harmonically conceived but the result was a harmonic accompaniment; this transformation from contrapuntal to harmonic writing is one of the reasons basso continuo came into being.

---

[3] Franciscus Bossinensis (Franjo Bosanac), *Tenori e contrabbassi intabulati col sopran in canto figurato per cantar e sonar col lauto* (Venice, 1509 and Fossombrone, 1511).

[4] Quoted by Federico Mompellio, 'Un certo ordine di procedere che non si può scrivere', *Scritti in onore di Luigi Ronga* (Milan and Naples, 1973), pp. 367–88.

[5] See William Prizer, 'Courtly Pastimes: The Frottole of Marchetto Cara', in George Buelow (ed.), *Studies in Musicology*, vol. 33 (Ann Arbor: UMI Research Press, 1980).

[6] See Howard Mayer Brown, *Instrumental Music Printed Before 1600* (Cambridge, MA, 1965) and Iain Fenlon and James Haar, *The Italian Madrigal in the Early Sixteenth Century* (Cambridge, 1988) for more detail on these publications.

Basso continuo began to be schematized at the beginning of the 1600s, yet harmonic accompaniments with the same characteristics as basso continuo are described from as early as 1550 and appear in the most musically influential cities of Italy.

Ortiz in the South of Italy in the 1550s

Diego Ortiz, born in Toledo, *maestro di cappella* at the Spanish court in Naples, was defined even by his contemporaries as 'per antichità napoletano' (Neapolitan since ancient times);[7] the accompaniments he describes are testimony to the period and place. His treatise, *Tratado de glosas sobre clausulas y otros generos de puntos en la musica de violones*, was published in Rome in 1553; his description of three ways to perform divisions on the *violone* encompass three different ways of accompanying on the harpsichord.

The first type of accompaniment he describes as a *Fantasia*; the musical examples that follow have no bass line. This type of accompaniment is the most difficult to recreate as there is no example of what the keyboard would have played; clearly an improvisation is implied.

> *Dechiaratione della maniere che s'han da sonare col Violone, e col Cimbalo insieme.*
> In questo secondo Libro si trattano le varie maniere che si debbano sonare col Violone, e col Cimbalo inseme. Tre sonno li maniere di sonare. La Prima si dice Fantasia. La Seconda sopra canto Piano. La Terza sopra compositione di molte voci. La Fantasia non si può mostrare, che ciascuno buon sonatore la suona di sua testa e di suo studio e uso ma ben dirò quel che si richieda per sonarla. La fantasia che sonerà il Cimbalo sia di consonanze ben ordinate ove poi entri sonando il Violone con alcuni leggiadri passaggi. E quando el Violone si trattiene in alcune tirate overo archate piane, allhora il Cimbalo gli risponda a proposto. E insieme faccino alcune fughe belle havendo riguardo e rispetto l'un all'altro ...

> [In this second book the various ways in which the *violone* and harpsichord should play together are dealt with. There are three ways of playing. The first is called *Fantasia*. The second is above a plainchant. The third above a composition for many voices. The *Fantasia* cannot be shown, as every good player performs this in their own manner through study and practice, but I will say what is required to play it. The *fantasia* that the harpsichord plays should be made up of well-ordered consonances, then the *violone* should enter playing some charming passages; when the *violone* plays some runs or long notes then the harpsichord should answer appropriately, and together they should play some fugues, with regard and respect for one another ...]

---

[7]   Scipione Cerreto, *Della prattica musica vocale e strumentale* (Naples, 1601), p. 158, quoted in Marco di Pasquale's introduction to the S.P.E.S. facsimile edition (Florence, 1984).

The second type of accompaniment he describes is effectively basso continuo: the bass line is given, and must be realized with appropriate harmonies as well as a little counterpoint befitting the *violone* part. He describes it thus:

> *De la seconda manera de tener el Violon con el Cymbalo que es sobre canto Ilano.*
> Desta manera de tañer pongo aqui. 6. Reçercadas sobre este canto llano quese sigue, elqual se ha de poner enel Cymbalo por donde esta apuntado por contrabaxo, acompañandole con consonançias y algun contrapunto al proposito de la Recercada que tañera el Violon destas seys ...

> [*On the second way of playing the violone with the harpsichord over a plainchant*
> Of this way of playing I put here 6 *Recercadas* on this plainchant that follows, and the harpsichord should play what is written for the bass, accompanying with consonances and some counterpoint appropriate to the *Recercada* the *violone* is playing ...]

The ricercares that follow have a bass line at the beginning of the piece, with the *violone* part printed underneath (Example 2.1).

RECERCADA PRIMERA.

Example 2.1 **D. Ortiz,** *Tratado de glosas,* **'Recercada primera'**

Clearly the melodic interest lies with the solo part and the realization of the bass must be supportive and simple, as this is the plainchant. The chords, mostly

$^5_3$ root positions, can occasionally be decorated with a passing note when moving from one chord to the next.

Ortiz then goes on to discuss three further ways of playing divisions of the madrigal on the *violone*; the harpsichord is to play the madrigal itself, which here is set out in 'choirbook' layout on two pages (Example 2.2):

> Hase de tomar el Madrigal, o Motete, o otra qualquier obra que se quisiere tanner, y ponerla enel cimbalo, como ordinariamente se suele hazer, y el q̃ tañe el Violon puede tañer sobre cada cosa compuesta dos o tres differentias, o mas. A qui pongo quattro sobre este Madrigal q̃ se sigue. La primera es el mismo contrabaxo de la obra con algunas glosas y algunos passos largos. La segunda manera es el suprano glosado, y en esta manera de tañer tiene mas gracia q̃ el q̃ tañe el cymbalo no taña el suprano ...

> [The madrigal, or motet, or whatever else one wishes to play, should be set for the harpsichord as ordinarily happens [i.e. intabulated], and above [this setting] the *violone* can play two or three, or more, divisions. Here I give four [divisions] of the madrigal that follows. The first is the same bass line of the work with some fast passages and some slow passages. The second way is to have the divisions in the soprano, in which case it would be more graceful if the harpsichord did not play the soprano line ...]

Here the keyboard player is instructed to play simply the four parts of the madrigal while the *violone* makes divisions. Should these divisions be of the bass line, the keyboard player must nonetheless play the madrigal as written; if the divisions are of the soprano line, the keyboard player is asked to omit that voice, playing only the three lower voices.

Ortiz has described the three main ways in which accompaniments were played: through improvisation, with a chordal accompaniment (basso continuo), and by playing the voices of an intabulated madrigal (the most common means of accompaniment before basso continuo).

Ferrara, 1570s

In the late sixteenth century Ferrara was, of course, famous for the female singers at the Gonzaga court; as well as singing, Laura Peperara, Livia d'Arco and Anna Guarini played, together with their music master Luzzasco Luzzaschi and the Maestro Fiorini. The chronicler Don Girolamo Merenda recounts the musical scene at court:

> Ed ogni giorno il tempo d'estate, il dopo desinare cominciano a cantare ... l'organista con lo arpicordo, il signor Fiorino con il lauto grosso, la signora Livia con la viola, la signora Guarina con un lauto, e la signora Laura con l'arpa.[8]

---

[8]   Quoted by Adriano Cavicchi in the introduction to his edition of Luzzasco Luzzaschi's *Madrigali per cantare et sonare* (Brescia, 1965).

Example 2.2 D. Ortiz, *Tratado de glosas*, 'O felici occhi miei'

[And every day in summertime, after dinner they start singing ... the organist at the harpsichord, Signor Fiorino with the big lute, Signora Livia with the *viola*, Signora Guarina with a lute, and Signora Laura with the harp.]

However, as Cavicchi points out, no music from the Ferrarese court that calls for this instrumentation has survived in manuscripts or printed music; but an example of how Luzzaschi might have been accompanying on his own, on the harpsichord, is illustrated in his Madrigals published in 1601 (Example 2.3).[9]

The Medici ambassador to the court, Bernardo Canigiani, in a letter of 13 August 1571 to the Grand Duke of Tuscany, writes: 'dentro [al suono di] un gravicembolo tocco dal Luciasco, cantorno la signora Lucrezia e la signora Isabella Bendedio a solo a solo, e tutt'a due, sì bene et così gentilmente che io non credo che si possa sentir meglio' [Accompanied on the harpsichord by Luciasco, Signora Lucrezia and Signora Isabella Bendedio solo and together sang so well and delicately I do not believe it possible to hear better'].[10]

The accompaniments to Luzzasco Luzzaschi's *Madrigali*, like most written-out accompaniments, have a very precise function. Rather than thinking of these as being any kind of realization it is important to bear in mind that these are madrigals; the harpsichord part is the *intavolatura* of the madrigal, therefore when one voice is singing the harpsichord doubles it, and when three voices are singing the harpsichord doubles them all, adding only the bass line. The result is most successful because these are madrigals composed to be written in an *intavolatura* so, unlike many vocal madrigals that are ruined when forced into an *intavolatura*, these have correct voice-leading and are comfortable to play. The idea of writing a madrigal to be written in *intavolatura* is not new in the 1570s, indeed it is what Ortiz was describing (see pp. 8–10). However, these Ferrarese madrigals are most extraordinary because of their written-out, and printed, vocal ornamentation, in true Ferrarese taste; the way the harpsichord responds to these ornamented passages is to play a simplified version of what is being sung. This is an effect that would be sought again in organ accompaniments when sacred vocal music became more ornamented in the first decade of the 1600s (discussed on pp. 55–7).

It is from Ferrara that one of the first testimonies to basso continuo comes. Striggio wrote to the Grand Duke in 1584 about a new composition of his: 'havevo ancora scritto la intavolatura per il lautto et me lo scordai in Mantova nel mio partire. Ma importarà poco, poichè il sig. Giulio [Caccini] potrà benissimo sonare, o con il lautto, o con il cembalo sopra il basso' ['I had written the *intavolatura* for the lute and forgot it in Mantova during my departure. But it will not matter much because Signor Giulio [Caccini] will be able to play perfectly well with the lute or the harpsichord over the bass'].[11] Clearly, specifically to play 'con il

---

9   Luzzasco Luzzaschi, *Madrigali per cantare et sonare* (Rome, 1601).
10   Quoted in Elio Durante and Anna Martellotti, *Cronistoria del concerto* (Florence, 1989), p. 130.
11   Quoted in Durante and Martellotti, *Cronistoria del concerto*, p. 164.

Example 2.3　　**L. Luzzaschi,** *Madrigali,* **'Aura soave'**

cembalo sopra il basso' was quite a new and relatively rare art; Caccini's arrival and skill seems to be the cause of some excitement, worth remarking that he can play from the bass alone. Caccini lived and worked in Florence where one of the most important of musical revolutions was taking place, in which accompanying instruments played a considerable part.

The Florentine Camerata

As well as the purely musical developments described up to now there were, indirectly, theoretical reasons why basso continuo emerged. Concern was raised by the musicians and theoreticians of the Florentine Camerata that words and poetry, obliged by the rules of counterpoint to fit and adapt to the musical phrase, had lost all their meaning in the polyphonic madrigal. The most important compositional consideration for the Camerata was the unity of text and music for, they argued, in antiquity the same person was poet and musician, singing to the accompaniment of one instrument. In this way expression was exalted; in Greek tragedy only one voice delivered the discourse.

This 'new style' of composition with one voice and accompaniment was being practised well before the 1600s; the first accounts of musical activities in Bardi's house date from 1573, although such activities were 'not formally chartered or organized'.[12] Even before that, in 1560, Bardi was sponsoring Galilei's study in Venice with Zarlino. In 1572–73 Galilei and Bardi were corresponding with Mei about Greek tragedy. In the Preface to *L'Euridice*, Caccini says he was composing songs 'in the new manner' as early as 1585.

The work of the Camerata is well known and extensively researched,[13] yet it is worth considering the role of the accompanying instruments in this new style of writing, as well as to what extent their role affected the new style: accompaniments were now consciously being written and performed in a harmonic fashion, rather than harmonic accompaniments being the inadvertent result of crushed counterpoint.

The Rejection of Contrapuntal Accompaniments

In the Preface to *Le nuove musiche*,[14] Caccini states that counterpoint is no longer needed in either composition or performance of this music. Most revealingly he writes:

> alla buona maniera di comporre, e cantare in quello stile serve molto di più l'intelligenza del concetto, e delle parole il gusto, e l'imitazione di esso così nelle corde affettuose, come nello esprimere con affetto cantando, che non serve il contrappunto, essendomi io servito di esso per accordar solo le due parti insieme.

> [to compose and sing well in that style it is more useful to have an understanding of the concept, and taste of the words, and imitate these both in the notes [of the accompaniments] with *affetto*, as well as when singing with *affetto*; counterpoint is not necessary, indeed I used it only to make the two parts agree.]

---

[12]   Claude Palisca, *The Florentine Camerata* (New Haven, CT, and London, 1989).

[13]   See Palisca, *The Florentine Camerata*, for a detailed discussion of the theoretical principals of the Florentine Camerata, as well as reproductions of original texts.

[14]   Giulio Caccini, *Le nuove musiche* (Florence, 1601), Preface.

The harmonies and inner voices are left to the continuo player and are no longer governed by the composer; now, the continuo performance is more important as a means of expression than the composition itself, and the performer takes on part of the role of the composer. This music is not contrapuntally composed; and neither should its accompaniment be contrapuntal but harmonic and guided by the meaning of the words.

Giovanni de' Bardi says most beautifully why these songs need to be accompanied in this way by these instruments: 'Cantandosi solo, o in su'l liuto, o gravicembalo, o altro strumento si puote à suo piacere la battuta stringere, e allargare, avvenga che à lui stia guidare la misura à suo piacimento' ['Singing alone with a lute, or harpsichord, or other instrument, one can at one's pleasure quicken or lengthen the bar, as it is for him [the singer] to guide the beat as he pleases'].[15] Praise for continuo playing and the freedom it allows is recurring in the surviving descriptions of the new style of the Camerata; a freedom acquired in no small part through the possibilities for responsiveness to the voice part given by this form of notation, underlining the importance of the Camerata's role in developing basso continuo accompaniment. For the success of the *stile rappresentativo* a means of accompaniment that freed the singer completely to conjoin words and music was necessary. When reading from basso continuo the accompanist can support the voice and change the texture and, consequently, the volume according to the *affetti* required by the words. With the *stile rappresentativo* becoming the most refined and sought-after musical form, basso continuo as the most versatile type of accompaniment was wholly appropriate to performance that specifically defined itself by its ornate, expressive eloquence – in the voice, through the use of *sprezzatura*, but in the accompaniment as well. For this reason the Camerata chose to use and develop it; the changes of the *nuovo stile* were as all-encompassing as was its success.

A characteristic of the music of the Camerata was to have one instrument accompanying one voice.[16] Severo Bonini gives descriptions of how two of the leading musicians of the Camerata, Giulio Caccini and Jacopo Peri, accompanied. Of Caccini he writes: 'sino a quei tempi non avevano mai udito armonia d'una voce sola sopra uno strumento semplice di corde che avesse avuto tanta forza di muover l'affetto dell'animo quanto quei madrigali' ['until that time they had never heard such harmony of one voice above a simple instrument with strings that had such power to move the feelings of the soul as those madrigals']. And of Peri writes: 'Questo sol ben dirò, che se fu suavissimo nel canto e perito nell'arte del

---

15 Giovanni de' Bardi, *Discorso mandato da Gio. de' Bardi a Giulio Caccini detto Romano sopra la musica antica, e il cantar bene*, reproduced in Giovanni Battista Doni, *De' trattati di musica*, vol. II (Florence, 1763), p. 246.

16 With the exception of the very first performance, when Vincenzo Galilei sang his own composition, a setting of Dante's *Lamento del Conte Ugolino*, to the accompaniment of five viols. See Pietro de' Bardi, *Lettera a G.B. Doni sull'origine del melodramma*, 1634, quoted in Solerti, *Le origini del melodramma* (Turin, 1903), pp. 144–5.

comporre in questo nuovo stile, fu ancora nell'arte del sonare di tasti leggiadro e artifizioso e, nell'accompagnare il canto con le parti di mezzo, unico e singolare' ['I will say only this, if he was the smoothest in song and expert in the art of composing in this new style, he was more so in the art of playing the keyboard gracefully and skilfully and, when accompanying the voice with the middle parts, unique and remarkable'].[17]

Vincenzo Giustiniani also notes that at this time the accompaniment was played by one instrument alone: 'L'anno santo del 1575 o poco dopo si cominciò un modo di cantare molto diverso da quello di prima, e così per alcuni anni seguenti, massime nel modo di cantare con una voce sola sopra un istrumento' ['In the holy year of 1575 or a little later there began a manner of singing very different from the earlier, thus it was for many subsequent years, the height of fashion to sing with a single voice over one instrument'].[18]

Giovanni Battista Doni comments similarly that only one instrument was used to accompany the songs, and comments on Caccini's style: 'Era in quel tempo nella Camerata del sig. Giovanni, Giulio Caccini, romano, di età giovanile, ma leggiadro cantore e spiritoso; il quale, sentendosi inclinato a tal sorte di musica, molto vi si affaticò, componendo e cantando molte cose al suono di un istrumento solo, che per lo più era una tiorba ...' ['In the Camerata of Signor Giovanni at that time was Giulio Caccini, a Roman, young but a skilled singer and full of spirit; who, feeling inclined to that kind of music, worked hard at it, composing, and singing many things to the sound of one instrument, which more often than not was a theorbo ...'].[19]

The influence of this music was far-reaching. The works were to become some of the most famous in Italy, as well as abroad, and the style was carried throughout the peninsula in the travels of the musicians involved in the Camerata and the music of the courts.

Works for Larger Forces

The new style of composing and performing was being applied to larger scale works by the end of the 1580s. The intermezzo *La Pellegrina*, performed by the leading musicians of the Camerata in 1589, was a combination of the old and new style; polyphonic madrigals were sung alongside songs written in the *nuovo stile*.[20] Different types of notation were used depending on the type of music that was

---

[17] Severo Bonini, *Discorsi e regole sopra la musica*, ed. L. Galleni Luisi (Cremona, 1975), pp. 106–7, 109.

[18] Vincenzo Giustiniani, *Discorso sopra la musica de' suoi tempi* (1628), quoted in Solerti, *Le origini del melodramma*, p. 106.

[19] Giovanni Battista Doni, *Trattato della musica scenica*, in *Trattati di musica*, vol. II, p. 23.

[20] See Nino Pirrotta, *Li due Orfei: da Poliziano a Monteverdi* (Turin, 1975) for a detailed discussion of these, as well as previous, *intermedi*.

accompanied and both *intavolature* and basso continuo were represented in one work; here, where the new style of accompaniment was applied to larger forces, many instruments accompanied together from basso continuo notation.

At the end of the century comments begin to appear criticizing the manner in which these newly formed continuo 'orchestras' were playing. Ercole Bottrigari, in 1594, writes of a performance held in Bologna:

> vi era un Clavicembalo grande, e una Spinetta grande, Tre Lauti di varie forme, una grande quantità di Viuole, e un'altra di Tromboni, due Cornetti un dritto, e uno torto; due Ribechini, e alquanti Flauti grossi, diritti, e traversi; un'Arpa doppia grande e una Lira tutti per l'accompagnamento di molte buone voci.[21]

> [There was a large harpsichord and a large spinet, three lutes of various shapes, a large quantity of *viole*, and of trombones, two cornetts one straight and one curved; two *ribechini*, and a certain number of big *flauti*, *diritti* and *traversi*; a large *arpa doppia* and a *lira* all for the accompaniment of many good voices.]

The manner of their performance was unsatisfactory to him, as he complains:

> tutti muoversi, come à garra in un tempo medesimo à far passaggi ... ne succede una insopportabile confusione; la quale tanto maggiormente si accresce all'hora che anco quelli ... che essercitano la parte grave, e bassa, non si ricordano ... che ella è la base, e il fondamento, sopra il quale è stata fabbricata quella cantilena.

> [They all play at the same time as if in competition, to make *passaggi* [divisions] ... unbearable confusion ensues, which is increased as even those ... that are playing the deepest and lowest part forget ... that this is the base and the foundation, above which the songs are written.]

Bottrigari's 'unbearable confusion' is already referring, in 1594, to the problems of 'uncontrolled' continuo realization; already it had became necessary for composers to set guidelines on how the bass should be realized and the manner in which instruments should play together. Even more telling is Bottrigari's final sentence, illustrating the changes that were occurring between the sixteenth and seventeenth centuries: now, everything is composed above the bass, which is the foundation of the composition. There is no more complex counterpoint, but harmonically conceived compositions that continuo players must learn to realize.

---

[21] Ercole Bottrigari, *Il desiderio, o vero de' concerti di varij strumenti musicali* (Venice, 1594), p. 50.

Chapter 3

The Early Seventeenth Century

The Establishment of Basso Continuo

A stream of publications from 1600–02 dates the beginning of the codification of basso continuo, coinciding precisely with the development of the *stile rappresentativo* and the breaking away from contrapuntal polyphony in accompaniment. The most famous of these works are Viadana's *Cento concerti ecclesiastici*, 1602, for sacred music; Peri and Caccini's *Le musiche sopra L'Euridice*, published 1600–01 and Cavalieri's *Rappresentatione di Anima, et di Corpo*, 1600, for opera and large-scale works; and Caccini's *Le nuove musiche*, 1602, for solo songs.[1] In these works ample introductions to the interpretation of this new music were provided, meeting the need to facilitate performance, which had scant place in theoretical treatises. The treatises that best discuss practical issues related to basso continuo accompaniment include Agazzari's *Del sonare sopra 'l basso con tutti li stromenti*, 1607; Bianciardi's *Breve regola per imparar' a sonare sopra il basso*, 1607; Banchieri's *Conclusioni nel suono dell'organo*, 1609; all these texts praise, raise problems and open up polemics on this new way of accompanying.[2]

The bass line, both in its composition and execution, played an important role in the success of a piece. This is illustrated by what composers wrote in these introductions to their publications. Jacopo Peri, in the Introduction to *Le musiche sopra L'Euridice*, talks of the composition of the bass in relation to the *affetti*: 'feci muovere il Basso ... hor più, hor meno, secondo gli affetti' ['I made the bass move ... now more now less, as the *affetti* required'].[3]

Caccini, in the Preface to *Le nuove musiche*, writes that the middle parts, the realization itself, can express *affetti*: '... con le parti di mezzo tocche dall'istrumento per esprimere qualche affetto, non essendo buone per altro'

---

[1]   Ludovico Viadana, *Cento concerti ecclesiastici a una, a due, a tre, e quattro voci. Con il basso continuo per sonar nell'organo* (Venice, 1602); Jacopo Peri, *Le musiche sopra l'Euridice* (Florence, 1600); Giulio Caccini, *L'Euridice* (Florence, 1600); Emilio de' Cavalieri, *Rappresentatione di Anima, et di Corpo* (Rome, 1600); Caccini, *Le nuove musiche* (Florence, 1601).

[2]   Agostino Agazzari, *Del sonare sopra 'l basso con tutti li stromenti* (Siena, 1607); Francesco Bianciardi, *Breve regola per imparar' a sonare sopra il basso* (Siena, 1607); Adriano Banchieri, *Conclusioni nel suono dell'organo* (Bologna, 1608).

[3]   Peri, *Le musiche sopra l'Euridice*.

['... with the middle parts played by the instrument to express an *affetto*, as they serve no other purpose'].[4]

Agazzari writes of the harmonies to be used in the realization: 'dove sono le parole, bisogna vestirle di quell'armonia convenievole, che faccia, ò dimostri quell'affetto' ['where there are words, it is necessary to clothe them with suitable harmony that shows or demonstrates the *affetto*'].[5]

The harmonies should reflect the *affetti* implied by the words – as Doni goes on to explain: 'una terza minore nel grave induce certa mollizie, e una maggiore certa allegria, e vivacità, e alcune legature ti passano l'anima' ['a low minor third induces such softness, and a major such happiness and vivacity, whilst certain ties [dissonances] sear the soul'].[6]

The quick and enhancing response to the vocal line the accompanist could now play with was the most important and innovative feature of the new style of accompaniment. Basso continuo notation allowed the performer to vary the texture of the chords, the range the realization was played in, the speed at which the chords were spread, in response to each different interpretation. Contemporary accounts illustrate that the continuo player used the notation in this way; intuitively, many performers do the same today.

Agazzari writes: 'in conserto, servendo l'Organista per fondamento, deve suonare con molto giuditio havendo riguardo alla quantità, e qualità delle voci, e stromenti, essendo poche, usare poco registro, e consonanze, essendo quantità aggiungere, e scemar secondo, che l'occasione ricerca' ['in ensemble playing, when the organist's role is to serve as the foundation [bass], he must play with great judgement considering carefully the quantity and quality of the voices and instruments; if these are few, he must use only a quiet register, and few consonances; if there are many he must increase and diminish according to what the occasion requires'].[7]

Puliaschi describes the same style of continuo playing: 'soglio accompagnar la mia voce con diversa maniera di consonanze quando più piene, e quando più vote secondo il passo; in particolare quando la parte ch'io canto discende sotto il Basso da sonare mi servo di poche consonanze, e quelle che più accompagnano quel passo' ['I accompany my voice with different sorts of consonances, sometimes full and sometimes light according to the passage; in particular when the part that I sing descends beneath the played Bass, I use just a few consonances, those that best accompany that passage'].[8]

---

4   Caccini, *Le nuove musiche*.

5   Agazzari, *Del sonare sopra 'l basso con tutti li stromenti*, p. 5.

6   Doni, *Trattato della musica scenica*, in *De' trattati di musica*, II (Florence, 1763), p. 110.

7   Agostino Agazzari, *Copia d'una lettera scritta dal Sig. Agostino Agazzari à un virtuoso Sanese suo compatriotto*, in Adriano Banchieri, *Conclusioni nel suono dell'organo* (Bologna, 1609).

8   Giovanni Domenico Puliaschi, *Musiche varie a una voce con il suo basso continuo per sonare* (Rome, 1618).

Caccini encourages exactly the same technique (p. 14): to play more or fewer notes in the chords of the accompaniment depending on the writing of a particular passage. Further, the register and number of voices, their quality, the *affetti* conveyed, and the number of other continuo instruments that are also realizing the bass are the most important indicators for adapting the accompaniment to suit the situation.

Transposition

Transposition, too, was made easier by the use of basso continuo; it was common for songs and instrumental pieces to be transposed to suit a particular singer or instrument. This practice is widely documented, both in treatises and in introductions to song books; Bianciardi writes: 'molte volte occorre [trasportare i tuoni], ò per commodo de' cantori, ò per concertare con altri strumenti' ['often it is necessary [to transpose], for the comfort of the singers or for playing with other instruments'].[9]

Caccini specifies that his songs should be sung in the key that the singer finds most comfortable:

> Sarà perciò utile avvertimento, che il professore di ques'arte poi che egli deve cantar solo sopra Chitarrone, ò altro strumento di corde senza essere forzato accomodarsi ad altri, che à se stesso si elegga un tuono, nel quale possa cantare in voce piena, e naturale per isfuggire le voci finte.[10]

> [It will be useful to bear in mind that he who professes this art, when he is to sing alone with a *chitarrone* or other stringed instrument, not being forced to accommodate any others but himself, should choose a key in which he can sing with a full, natural voice, avoiding false notes [out of his natural range].]

A transposition of a bass line with its appropriate chords is not as difficult as would be a complete transposition of an *intavolatura* accompaniment.

Notation

The need for a system of notation that could work in compositions for larger forces reinforced the ascendancy of basso continuo. In large-scale works different types of instruments needed to realize the bass in the manner most appropriate to their instrument while reading from the same part. With basso continuo notation, keyboard instruments, lutes, harps and strings could all play together from the same part, each responding both to what was being accompanied and the manner

---

9   Bianciardi, *Breve regola per imparar' a sonare sopra il basso*.
10   Caccini, *Le nuove musiche*, Preface.

in which it was being accompanied by the other musicians around them. Problems of tuning and reconciling improvisations ensued (pp. 40–42).

There was a need, too, for a quicker and easier way than a tablature both to read and to copy the accompaniment, especially for the accompaniment of multi-voiced church music. Many instruments were now playing and improvising together with the common goal of achieving maximum effects, subtleties of colour and sonority, in the enhancement of the music. Agazzari, writing in 1607, confirms these to be the reasons why this new style of accompaniment had been introduced:

> Per tre cagioni dunque è stato messo in uso questo modo: prima per lo stile moderno di cantar recitativo, e comporre: seconda per la commodità: terza per la quantità, e varietà d'opere, che sono necessarie al conserto. Della prima dico, che essendosi ultimamente trovato il vero stile d'esprimere le parole, imitando lo stesso ragionare nel meglior modo possibile; il che meglio succede, con una, ò poche voci ... non è necessario far spartitura, ò intavolatura; ma basta un basso con i suoi segni come abbiamo detto sopra. Ma se alcuno mi dicesse, che à suonar l'opere antiche piene di fughe, e contrapunti, non è bastevole il basso, à ciò rispondo, non esser in uso più simil cantilene ...
>
> La seconda cagione è la commodità grande; perchè con picciola fatica havete molto capitale per le occorrenze, oltre che chi desidera imparare à sonare, è sciolto dalla intavolatura, cosa à molti difficile e noiosa; anzi molto soggetta à gl'errori perche l'occhio, e la mente è tutta occupata in guardar tante parti massime venendo occasione di consertar all'improviso.
>
> La terza finalmente, che è la quantità dell'opere necessarie al conserto, mi pare sola bastevole ad introdurre simil commodità di sonare: poichè se si havessero ad intavolare, ò spartire tutte l'opere, che si cantano fra l'anno in una sola Chiesa di Roma; dove si fa professione di consertare, bisognerebbe all'Organista che havesse maggior libraria, che qual si voglia Dottor di legge: onde à molta ragione si è introdotto simil basso, col modo però sopradetto.[11]

[[Basso continuo] is used in this way for three reasons: first because of the modern style of singing and composing recitative; second, for convenience; third, because of the quantity and variety of materials required for performance. I say of the first that because recently the true way of expressing words has been found, imitating speech in the best way possible – which works best with one, or few voices ... it is not necessary to make a *spartitura* or *intavolatura*; a bass with its markings [figures] as discussed above will suffice. And if someone said to me that to play ancient works, full of fugues and counterpoint, the bass alone is not enough, I would answer that no one sings these things any more ...

The second reason is the great convenience; for with little effort you can have a great deal of resources for any occasion, and besides, those who wish to learn to play are freed from the *intavolatura*, which many find difficult and tiresome; prone, even, to cause mistakes since the eye and the whole mind are busy looking at many parts, especially when the occasion arises to sight read whilst playing with others.

The third reason, finally, the number of copies of the works necessary for the ensemble, seems to me enough to introduce such convenience in playing; because if

---

[11]   Agazzari, *Del sonare sopra 'l basso*, pp. 10–12.

you had to intabulate or make scores of all the works that are sung in a year in just one church in Rome where performance is a profession, the organist would need a larger library than a doctor of law; for these reasons such a bass was introduced, in the way described above.]

Depending on the nature of the music, whether sacred or secular, solo or multi-voiced, at the beginning of the 1600s there were three main types of notation appropriate for the different types of compositions that were existing side by side, both old and new. These were:

- *partitura*, where a bass line is given with solo parts above; *partitura* retains the same meaning in modern Italian and simply means a score. When reading from this, the accompanist would have been score-reading, playing each vocal or instrumental part as written. After the establishment of basso continuo they would have used the upper parts as a guide to which harmonies should be played, no longer doubling the voices (pp. 55–7).
- *intavolatura*, used mainly in sacred music, is an intabulation of all or most of the parts of a multi-voiced work reduced onto two staves; the task of writing out the *intavolatura* was generally left to the organist, and it would have been particularly useful when the piece was printed in separate part books and no score was available (pp. 51–4). As with the *partitura* in its first years of existence, the effect of this type of notation was that all the sung parts were doubled by the organist. The term *intavolatura* was also the name given to the notation of keyboard music generally, as well as that used by lutes and theorboes (discussed on pp. 31–3); the term is not used exclusively in connection with accompaniments.
- *accompagnamento*, the most generic term simply meaning accompaniment, refers to the bass line, with or without figures, and with no part placed above. This was basso continuo.

Sonorities

There were many ways in which the new style of composing influenced the style of accompaniment: a search for different sonorities began that led to experimentation with the stringing and even construction of instruments. The lutes of the *rinascimento* gave way to theorboes with bass strings for octave doubling; harpsichords that were strung with an eight- and a four-foot register were transformed into *cembali doppi*, their four-foot exchanged for an extra row of eight, or simply with the extra set of strings added, the increased tension on the soundboard creating dramatic changes to the sound. Further experiments were taking place with the sonorities of these accompanying instruments, putting metal strings on theorboes and harps, gut strings on harpsichords – or silk, silver and even gold strings; changing the plectra of harpsichords for different effects and using brass or leather instead of quill; and many more examples. The sonorities produced when these instruments played, alone and together, evinced great interest, and rules and examples of what should be played, how, and with what, were diffused both by direction in performance and by publication.

Figures

Figures and Harmony

In the *Avvertimento* to his *Le musiche sopra L'Euridice*, Jacopo Peri does not write about the interpretation of the bass, but gives a short yet comprehensive guide to harmonizing the bass line:

> Sopra la parte del basso, il diesis congiunto col 6. dimostra sesta maggiore, e la minore senza 'l diesis; il quale quando è solo, è contrassegno della terza, ò della decima maggiore: Et il b.molle, della terza, ò decima minore; e non si ponga mai, se non a quella sola nota, dove è segnato, quantunque piu ne fussero in una medesima Corda.[12]

> [Over the bass part, the sharp together with the number 6 indicates a major sixth, and without the sharp the minor sixth; [the sharp] on its own indicates the major third or tenth; and the flat, a minor third or tenth; and it should never be placed other than on the one note on which it is marked, even though there may be more [numbers] on the same note.]

This encapsulates in the simplest way effectively all that is needed to play a basso continuo of the music of this period; the harmonies used were so simple that a description such as this, giving instructions regarding only thirds and sixths, was enough, at least in the first few years of the existence of basso continuo accompaniment.

Music of this period can be harmonized by following a simple set of rules which may be summed up, and put into modern terms, as follows: all chords take a $\frac{5}{3}$ chord, except the instances when a $\frac{6}{3}$ should be played, which are:

1 on the 'leading note' in the bass. Essentially this is the rule of the octave for avoiding tritones. The concept of 'leading note' is anachronistic, but defines the situation clearly.
2 by extension, on any accidental sharp on the bass note, which includes an accidental natural cancelling a key-signature B♭; again, using modern terms.
3 on the middle note of three bass notes in a row.

---

[12] Peri, *Le musiche sopra l'Euridice*.

A 7 leading to a 6 is essentially a harmonic ornament of a 6; 7–6 can be played if there is time and the upper parts suit it. Passing notes should be identified, especially at cadence points, and should not all be harmonized.

Regarding final chords, Agazzari (and others) makes the generalization that these should be major: 'Tutte l'accadenze, ò mezzane, ò finali, voglion la terza maggiore, e però alcuni non le segnano' ['All cadences, whether in the middle or at the end [of a piece], take a major third, although some do not write this'].[13] When figures are not given, the third is not written in the parts, and there is no indication of whether the chords should be major or minor, then the continuo player becomes arbiter in the choice of chords to be played. Lack of figuring and widespread reliance on the harmonic knowledge of the performer began to be acknowledged within the first decade of the 1600s; probably because of the relative harmonic simplicity of this music, composers became less consistent in their figuring, leaving the realization entirely up to the continuo player, who was expected to be able to play the correct harmonies from reading the score (indeed, in some cases from the bass line alone) and not expected to need numbers to indicate the chord. Agazzari writes:

> Conchiudo che non si può dar determinata regola di suonar l'opere, dove non sono segni alcuni, conciosa che bisogna obedir la mente del compositore, quale è libera, e può, à suo arbitrio, sopra una nota nella prima parte di essa metter 5.a ò 6.a e per il contrario: e quella maggiore, ò minore, secondo gli par più à proposito, overo che sia necessitato à questo dalle parole.[14]

> [I conclude by saying that it is not possible to give rules on how to play pieces which have no signs [figures]; be aware that the composer's intention must be followed, as it is free and may, at his sole discretion, in the first part of a note, call for a 5 or a 6 or the reverse, or a major or minor chord depending which seems to him most appropriate or necessary for the words.]

Bianciardi comments similarly: 'resta nondimeno la libertà al compositore d'usar le consonanze à suo capriccio; cioè d'usar la sesta in luogo della quinta; e le terze minori in luogo delle maggiori; mescolando diverse spetie di dissonanze; delle quali il darne sicuro ordine, è impossibile' ['The composer remains free to use consonances at his whim; that is, using the sixth in the place of a fifth; minor thirds instead of major thirds; mixing different types of dissonances for which it would be impossible here to give a specific order'].[15] There was an unconcern in specifying more clearly what harmonies were intended; difficulties that arose for the continuo player when only an unfigured part-book was given to play from were not addressed. Franzoni, for example, does not leave many specific instructions to the organist, but refers them to Agazzari's treatise:

---

[13] Agazzari, *Del sonare sopra 'l basso*, p. 6.
[14] Agazzari, *Del sonare sopra 'l basso*, p. 4.
[15] Bianciardi, *Breve regola*.

Havrei potuto nel presente Basso notare alcune Conzonanze, e dissonanze per rendere più facile il sonare la present' opera, ma à bello studio l'ò tralasciato per non far torto à signori Organisti, quali col loro purgato orecchio sapranno secondare la composizione co' i loro leggiadri movimenti. Tanto piu havendone à bastanza, e gratiosamente di ciò discorso Agostino Agazaro, nel Secondo Libro de suoi Concerti, alquale io mi riporto.[16]

[In this bass I could have marked some consonances and dissonances in order to make it easier playing this work, but I have avoided this deliberately in order not to offend our gentlemen organists who, with their refined ear, will be able to gratify the composition with their beautiful way of playing. All the more so since Agostino Agazaro discussed all this sufficiently and most eloquently in the second book of his *Concerti*, to which I refer.]

Agazzari, however, does not give an exhaustive explanation of how to harmonize unfigured bass lines in his treatise. His own advice to performers is exemplified in the introduction to his own *Sacrae cantiones*, where he advises the organist to study the score well and figure the part accordingly:

voglio avvertire quel che suona, che per mancanza della stampa non havendo potuto segnare li ♯ e li ♭, cioè le terze maggiori, e minori, e i numeri sopra le note conforme al bisogno loro, vogli porger l'orecchio à i cantanti, e secondar la tessitura, se già non volesse segnarli con la penna rivedendoli prima …[17]

[I want to warn the player, that because of printing problems I have been unable to mark the ♯ and ♭, that is the major and minor thirds, and the numbers above the notes according to their needs; please therefore keep your ear out for the singers, favour the tessitura, and perhaps mark them [the figures] in pen, checking first that they are right …]

This is one of the very few instances where figures are said to have been omitted because of printing difficulties; also it is exceptional that Agazzari should advise the organist to write the numbers in with a pen; advice actually carried out by the organist who played from the organ part of the 1614 print, held in the British Library.[18] There are indeed figures written in pen, on pages 6, 10, 11 and 13; '♯' is marked frequently, and '3 4 3', sometimes '4 3', is written at cadence points.

Brunetti writes that all the organist need do is consider the note preceding and the note following the one he is playing, as well as listen to the vocal part, to work out what harmonies should be played: 'Non ho voluto mettervi abachi per gli accompagnamenti prosuponendo [sic] che l'Organista havendo risguardo alle note antecedente e sussequente, con dare anco orecchia alle parti che cantano;

---

[16]   Amante Franzoni, *Concerti ecclesiastici* (Venice, 1611), 'A' benigni lettori'.

[17]   Agostino Agazzari, *Sacrae cantiones* (Venice, 1608), *Liber quartos*.

[18]   Agazzari, *Sacrae cantiones, liber quartos, bassus ad organum* part-book, GBLbl C.30.K.

possi facilmente venire in cognitione dalle loro relationi gli accompagnamenti che se li devono' ['I did not wish to put numbers for the accompaniment assuming that the organist, if he looks at the note before and after, and listens well to the parts that are singing, can easily work out, by their relation, which accompaniments he should be giving'].[19]

This paucity of figures is a characteristic of Italian music that was never to be altered. Indeed, when more detailed treatises on basso continuo begin to appear towards the end of the seventeenth century, all concentrate on explaining how to harmonize an unfigured bass. Many, as will be seen, begin to teach which unwritten harmonies should be played, and which notes can then be added to the simple harmonic framework to add colour (pp. 71–3).

Figures and style

The introductions to the first Florentine operas contain precious information on the realization of the bass; a consideration of these instructions is invaluable for an understanding of the requirements of the style. The indications on continuo playing are closely tied with comments on how the music is composed and the *affetti* expressed in the vocal line. In the early operas composers leave the finer, delicate points of interpretation up to the performer, combining basic explanations on how to read figures with confident expressions of reliance, and compliments, on the good taste of the performer. Certainly the performers would not have been inexperienced organists and harpsichordists who did not know well how to accompany. However, this being a new style of accompaniment for a new style of music and these keyboard players probably coming from the *intavolatura* tradition, they had to be told relatively basic things about the *nuovo stile*: that it is not necessary to play the consonances that are being sung, that it is desirable to play without decoration, and that it is important to keep the harmony alive, although not by introducing counterpoint or ornamentation.

Many stylistic matters are discussed by Marco da Gagliano in his Preface to *La Dafne*.[20] Gagliano specifies that the continuo players should be able to see the singers in order to be able to accompany them better; a rare indication of practical placing in performance, indicating the high level of interaction and precision demanded from the continuo players. On the realization of the bass, he writes that the player should not 'restrike the sung consonances' – that is, not double the vocal line – but support the voice by keeping the harmony alive. This style of playing is aided by basso continuo notation.

Primieramente avvertiscasi che gli strumenti, che devono accompagnare, le voci sole, sieno situati in luogo, da vedere in viso i recitanti accio che meglio sentendosi vadano unitamente: procurisi, che l'armonia non sia ne troppa ne poca, ma tale che

---

19 Giovanni Brunetti, *Salmi intieri concertati à 5 e 6* (Venice, 1625).
20 Marco da Gagliano, *La Dafne* (Florence, 1608).

regga il canto senza impedire l'intendimento delle parole: il modo di sonare sia senza adornamenti, avendo riguardo di non riperquotere la consonanza cantata, ma quelle che più possono aiutarla mantenendo sempre l'armonia viva.

[First, ensure the instruments that accompany the voices are situated in a place so as to be able to see the singer's face so that, hearing each other better, they might play together; ensure that the harmony is neither too much nor too little, but such as to sustain the singing without preventing the understanding of words; the way of playing should be without ornament, taking care not to repeat the sung consonance, but to play those [consonances] which can best help, always keeping the harmony alive.]

The need for the greatest care in achieving balance between allowing the singers freedom and keeping to an elegant accompaniment imbues this text.

Caccini, in his Preface to *L'Euridice*, gives an invaluable practical indication: when a bass note is tied the inner parts should move according to the rhythmic division of the bass-note (Example 3.1). In this way Caccini illustrates the timing of the inner parts, specifying that the bass note itself should not be restruck:

Reggesi adunque l'armonia delle parti, che recitano nella presente Euridice sopra un basso continuato, nel quale ho io segnato le quarte, seste, e settime; terze maggiori, e minori più neccessarie rimettendo nel rimanente lo adattare le parti di mezzo à lor luoghi nel giudizio, e nell'arte di chi suona, havendo legato alcune volte le corde del basso, affine che nel trapassare delle molte dissonanze, ch'entro vi sono, non si ripercuota la corda, e l'udito ne venga offeso.[21]

[Hold therefore the harmony of the parts, which sing in this Euridice over a basso continuo, in which I have marked the fourths, sixths and sevenths, and the most necessary major and minor thirds; regarding the adaptation and placing of the middle parts, this is left to the judgement and art of the player, the bass notes sometimes being tied, to avoid, in the many passing dissonances which are there, that these notes be struck again, thus offending the ear.]

Example 3.1   G. Caccini, *L'Euridice*

---

[21]   Caccini, *L'Euridice* (Florence, 1600), Preface.

Caccini was not alone in using this system of notation, and Cavalieri, in the *Rappresentazione di Anima, et di Corpo*, even placed ties between numbers to show precisely when inner parts were tied, despite the movement or different rhythm of the bass (Example 3.2).

Example 3.2   E. Cavalieri, *Rappresentazione di Anima, et di Corpo*

Cavalieri explains how to harmonize the bass line: 'Li numeri piccoli posti sopra le note del Basso continuato per suonare, significano la Consonanza, ò Dissonanza di tal numero: come il 3. terza: il 4. quarta: e cosi di mano in mano' ['The small numbers placed above the basso continuo signify consonance or dissonance of that number; so 3 means a third, 4 is a fourth and so on']. 'Quando il diesis posto sopra le dette note, non è accompagnato con numero, sempre significa Decima maggiore' ['When the sharp sign is placed above these notes, and is not accompanied by a number, it always means a major tenth'].

Cavalieri's figuring ranges from 3 (or ♯) to 18 (used to indicate two octaves above a 4th). He is exceptionally exact with his figures, and his use of compound numbers is by no means arbitrary. A precise reading of his figuring gives indications for voice-leading; the highest instrumental part is often doubled by the figures, and the realization is never allowed to rise above the vocal part. Cavalieri seeks to control the continuo player's realization as much as the notation will allow.

Basso continuo uses a simple system of notation and its strength is its reliance on the performer to interpret the language; to dress this system with further meanings, as Cavalieri does, renders it less efficient. Figures used this way were sometimes indicators of tessitura as well as harmony; amongst others, Caccini, in *Le nuove musiche*, also uses both simple and compound figures. Banchieri, in his *Gemelli armonici*, consistently marks 3 in the pieces for tenor, and 10 in the pieces for soprano.[22]

Severo Bonini, in his *Madrigali e canzonette spirituali* of 1607, acknowledges differences of effect when the realization is by different instruments but he leaves the continuo player to interpret the score and realize the bass in the manner most appropriate to their instrument. He suggests that as compound figures are more

---

[22]   Adriano Banchieri, *Gemelli armonici* (Venice, 1609), A gli virtuosi musici.

appropriate to keyboard instruments than to the theorbo the bass line is best left *without* figures, so as to be played appropriately on both instruments:

> Benche oggidì in gran parte si stampino musiche per una voce sola come quelle, che sono state giudicate più atte, e di maggior forza à muovere l'affetto dell'animo, segnando sopra del Basso terze maggiori, e minori, seste, e altre legate hò voluto nondimeno segnare alcune terze maggiori più necessarie, non solo perché la parte che canta mostra dette seste, e altro, mà anco per lasciare in arbitrio di chi suona lo adattare à suo talento dette parti di mezzo, perchè altro effetto fanno le terze, e quarte sopra del chitarrone, e altro effetto le decime, e undecime sopra lo strumento de' tasti.[23]

> [Although nowadays, most commonly, music for one voice is printed marking above the bass major and minor thirds, sixths, and other ties, as this has been judged most apt and most effective in moving the state of the soul, nevertheless I have wished to mark some of the more important major thirds, not just because the voice part shows these sixths, and more but, also, to leave the player to judge how to adapt these middle parts according to his talents, for the effect of thirds and fourths on the *chitarrone* is one thing, and that of tenths and elevenths on the keyboard instrument is another.]

The type of figures printed by the composers could therefore depend on the voices accompanied and the instruments upon which the accompaniment was played; because of the theorbo's tuning the realization is in a lower register than that of keyboard instruments.

Bianciardi acknowledges:

> E' ben vero, che, usando le consonanze composte, e replicate, faremo più diversa l'armonia; cioè, se in luogo della terza, daremo la 10a e 17a, ed in luogo della quinta, la 12a e 19a e così l'altre. Ma, perché sarebbe troppo povera l'armonia, se solamente si ponessino le tre voci, sarà molto utile aggiunger dell'ottave al Basso, et all'altre parti per arricchirla, e dar luogo di passare da una consonanza all'altra più continuamente, con più leggiadria, e con maggior commodo della mano.[24]

> [It is true that, using compound and doubled consonances, we can make the harmony more varied; that is, if instead of a third, we played 10 and 17, and instead of a fifth, 12 and 19, and so on. Yet as the harmony would be too poor if we only played three voices, it will be very useful to add octaves to the bass, and to the other parts in order to enrich [the sound], and make it possible to pass from one consonance to another with more continuity, lightness, and convenience for the hand.]

Furthermore:

> Anzi che molte volte per necessità delle parole si ricerca pienezza di voci, e nell'esclamazioni aiuto co' le corde estreme; nelle materie allegre star nell'acuto, più

[23] Severo Bonini, *Madrigali e canzonette spirituali* (Florence, 1607).
[24] Bianciardi, *Breve regola*.

che si può; nelle meste star nel grave; nelle cadenze toccar l'ottave sotto al Basso; fuggendo nelle corde molto gravi le terze, e le quinte: perché fanno troppa borda l'armonia, offendendo l'udito.

[Indeed, often the words require that one looks for fullness of voices [full chords], and in *esclamazioni*, help from the lower notes. With joyful subjects it is best to stay as high as possible; in sad [pieces] stay low. At cadences play the octave below the bass, avoiding very low thirds and fifths as they render the harmony too dense, offending the ear.]

So, in performance the realization must display a variety of range in keeping with what has gone before, that sits comfortably under the hand, and that reflects and enhances the work.

Notation and Instrumentation

The guitar alphabet Problems of which harmonies to play did not arise with the use of the guitar alphabet, which publishers of song books often added to the score; the guitar was widely played because the alphabet, where each chord is represented by a letter, made the accompaniments of the songs accessible to larger numbers of players. The popularity of the guitar grew, in part, from the fact that its player did not have to be able to read music; only knowledge of the alphabet was needed to strum along with a song. The resulting accompaniment is almost purely harmonic; nonetheless, the alphabet has more than one letter for every chord, producing different distributions of notes;[25] arguably the exact choice of which chord follows which chord, both for convenience and for effect, promotes a certain voice-leading. Although it is not the alphabet that renders the accompaniment harmonic and, added by the publisher not the composer, there are often mistakes in the alphabet accompaniments, it is nevertheless a system that notates certain aspects that would not necessarily be notated in figures; harmonic choices are often surprising.

Girolamo Montesardo's *Hor che la nott'ombrosa* exemplifies certain harmonies that perhaps might be considered too striking today;[26] in Example 3.3a, the proximity of the G major and e minor chords is noteworthy. The guitar alphabet indicates, unusually, a minor chord at the end (Example 3.3b).

---

[25] As exemplified by Biagio Marini, *Scherzi e canzonette* (Parma, 1622).

[26] Girolamo Montesardo, *I lieti giorni di Napoli* (Naples, 1612). The examples are taken from Montesardo for, insofar as he claims to have invented the alphabet, the accompaniments in his music are more likely to have been supervised and corrected by the composer.

Example 3.3a   G. Montesardo, *I lieti giorni di Napoli*, 'Hor che la nott'ombrosa'

Example 3.3b   G. Montesardo, *I lieti giorni di Napoli*, 'Hor che la nott'ombrosa'

Intavolatura for chitarrone   Lutenists and theorbo players habitually read from *intavolature*. In relation to these instruments the term takes a different meaning from that used with reference to the keyboard and refers specifically to their tablature. In this system six lines each represent a string on the instrument; numbers are placed on the lines indicating which finger should be placed on which string.

As theorbo players often had more familiarity with reading their tablature than with reading standard notation, song books began to be published with the accompaniment written in theorbo tablature thereby providing, it might be assumed, a composed continuo part with each chord given exactly as it was intended it should be played; however, responsiveness to the singer and, necessarily following from this, the dynamics and density of the realization of the bass remained the most important features of the accompaniment and demanded a more complex response. Despite the theorbo having more dynamic possibilities than the harpsichord or organ it was still the case that basso continuo was the best way to accompany, for it specifically permitted the accompanist freely to change the number of notes per chord according to what was being sung. While accompaniments written in the form of theorbo *intavolature* can be taken as a testimony to a certain, simple way of accompanying it would be unwise to use them as a guide on how these songs were effectively accompanied by the theorbo players of the time; these written-out chordal accompaniments were provided for the less experienced player who perhaps could not read from the bass line.

Of course some theorbo *intavolature* are simpler than others; depending on the authorship of these accompaniments, and whether they were printed, and therefore aimed at a commercial public, or in manuscript, most probably intended for personal use, they can be more, or less, beautiful.

Written-out intavolatura accompaniments The Brussels Manuscript 704 is an example of the simple form of accompaniment, consisting of the most widely disseminated and copied popular songs of Caccini and Peri, among others, with a bass line and an *intavolatura* underneath.[27] The accompaniment is almost always purely harmonic, passing from one chord to another in the easiest positions for the hand, sacrificing any voice-leading; there is little invention and it is clearly written by, or aimed at, theorbo players with little experience in playing this type of accompaniment. It is not unlike the Florentine manuscript Magliabechi XIX 115 which has simple realizations of Caccini songs written out for harpsichord;[28] again purely harmonic and probably provided for the same kind of player, it is so simple and unelaborated, yet in a manner without grace and intent, that it can hardly be taken as indicative of the most desirable type of accompaniment of the time.[29]

Kapsberger's theorbo *intavolature* are far more interesting.[30] Some features of the accompaniment, such as syncopated rhythms and unprepared dissonances, add grace to the composition; yet a comparison with the solo theorbo music by Kapsberger, a great virtuoso of this instrument, suggests it is improbable that he would have performed such an accompaniment himself, for again it is an accompaniment that does not take into account contemporary requests for, as well as accounts of, subtlety and adaptability in continuo playing. Most importantly, however, it is hard to imagine such a player accompanying in so very simple, chordal a fashion. While much of his solo music, especially the *Toccate*, also can be broken down easily to the original harmonic framework, the difference between the composed Toccatas and these written-out realizations of the continuo line is so great that it is impossible to think of these *intavolature* accompaniments as a 'composed' continuo part; they too, most probably, are intended as an aid for those less familiar with continuo as a means of notation. So while the quality of Kapsberger's realizations remains superior to those of the Brussels and Florence

---

[27] *Musiche di vari autori* (BBc, MS 704).

[28] MS Magliabechi XIX 115 (IFn).

[29] See John Walter Hill, 'Realized continuo accompaniments from Florence c.1600', *Early Music*, vol. 11 (1983): 194–208, together with Robert Spencer's answer in in the following issue of *Early Music*, for a discussion of this manuscript.

[30] Johannes Hieronymus Kapsberger, *Libro primo di villanelle* (Rome, 1610); *Libro terzo di villanelle* (Rome, 1619); also *Libro primo di arie passeggiate à una voce con l'intavolatura del chitarrone* (Rome, 1612).

manuscripts, the availabilty of the composer's own realization of the bass should not exclude realization from the bass line, as the *intavolatura* is not an intrinsic and unalterable part of the composition as a whole. Bellerofonte Castaldi's theorbo *intavolature* are more ornate than those of Kapsberger; they too display a simple harmonic accompaniment, but with a little ornamentation, especially at cadence points.[31]

The widespread playing of the instrument by amateurs had led to published accompaniments, even those composed by the great theorbists of the time, being far simpler than sophisticated professional performers would have played.

It is in Robert Dowland's version of Caccini's *Amarilli mia bella* that it is possible to hear what a true composed accompaniment can sound like, adding to the vocal line with the composer's own ideas and making the whole accompaniment an integral part of the composition and no longer an improvisation. The *intavolature* for *chitarrone* by Italian composers and performers of the 1600s bear no resemblance to Dowland's compositional writing, yet the Italian solo repertoire of the period points to a level of virtuosity that surely would have been more present in accompaniment improvisation than these *intavolature* would lead us to believe, even given that an English version of an Italian madrigal cannot be taken as an example of Italian accompaniment. It is necessary to take into account the solo virtuoso writing for the instrument and the more general contemporary practices and expectations of accompaniment to understand what should be played, although a study of these notations, both the guitar alphabet and the *intavolature* for *chitarrone*, can sometimes surprise with their harmonies and instruct in their choices of voice-leading.

Scores of Solo Songs with More than One System of Notation

Song books began to be published with the voice part and any number of combinations of three different systems of accompaniment: the guitar alphabet, an *intavolatura* for the *chitarrone*, and a bass line with the voice part printed above. Flamminio Corradi's *Le stravaganze d'Amore* employs these three systems of notation (Example 3.4).[32]

There were problems, already raised (p. 17), in having different types of instruments playing the same bass line. Because of the disposition of the guitar's strings the lowest sounding note of a chord on the guitar might not be the bass note indicated in the score – often requiring an inversion of the marked chord to be played. This meant the guitar alphabet did not always correspond with the bass line – for example, a 6 chord on a B might have G as the lowest note on the guitar. This results in a richer accompaniment, and composers were not worried about changing the bass line in this way, as Marini acknowledges: 'Avvertino,

---

[31]   Bellerofonte Castaldi, *Capricci a due strumenti cioè tiorba e tiorbino* (Modena, 1622).

[32]   Flamminio Corradi, *Le stravaganze d'Amore, a una, due e tre voci* (Venice, 1616).

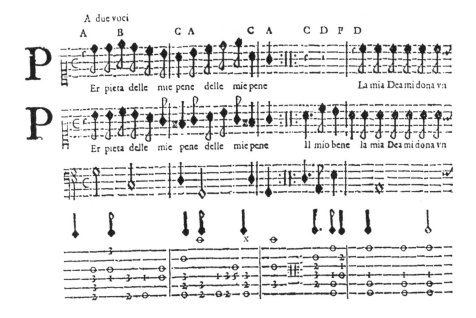

**Example 3.4   F. Corradi, *Le stravaganze d'amore*, 'Per pietà delle mie pene',
Bibliothèque nationale de France**

che se non troveranno in qualche loco di quest'opera l'Alfabetto concorde con
il Basso, l'animo dell'Autore è d'accompagnar la voce più che sij possibile, non
curandosi in questo d'obligarsi à quello, essendo la Chitariglia priva di molte
bone consonanze' ['Readers must bear in mind that, should they find some places
in this work where the alphabet does not agree with the bass, the intention of
the author is to accompany the voice as much as possible, without going to the
trouble of matching the former to the latter, since the *chitariglia* lacks many good
consonances'].[33]

Distinctions between the accompanying instruments began to be drawn, and
writing became more specific for each instrument:

Avvertendovi che per esser vario l'affetto, che rende il Chitarrone ò Spinetta, da quello
della Chitarra alla Spagnola nel sonar queste Ariette, in molti luoghi hò variata la
notta nella ditta Chitarra da quella, che è assignata nel Basso fondamentale, posta
per gl'altri stromenti, il tutto fatto per dar gli maggior vaghezza. Come anco non
si son posti li Diesis, ne signati i Numeri ne lor proprii luoghi del Basso Continuo,

---

[33] Marini, *Scherzi e canzonette*.

presupponendosi l'accortezza, e virtuosa maniera di colui, che le sonerà, havendo
l'occhio alla parte che canta.[34]

[The *affetto* rendered by the *chitarrone* or the spinet being different from that of the
chitarra alla spagnola in playing these arias, in many places I have changed the note
given to the *chitarra* from the one that is assigned in the *basso fondamentale*, for the
other instruments; all [of this is] to make it more beautiful. Also, sharps have not been
placed, nor numbers marked where expected in the basso continuo, taking for granted
the accomplishment and virtuosity of those who will play them, [while] at the same
time keeping an eye on the vocal line.]

Barbarino goes so far as to recommend which instruments sound best with which
voices, suggesting *chitarrone* for tenors and the harpsichord for sopranos:

Quei Madrigali, quali sono in chiave di soprano, si possono cantare in Tenore all'ottava
di sotto, che è veramente il suo proprio da cantare nel Chitarrone ò Tiorba che vogliam'
dire, che per commodità di chi suona di Clavecimbalo, e in particulare per le Dame mi
è parso metterle in detta chiave.[35]

[Madrigals in the soprano clef may be sung in the tenor an octave below, which is
actually how they should be sung when accompanied by the *chitarrone* or theorbo or
whatever one chooses to call it, so, for the benefit of those who play the harpsichord, and
notably for the Ladies, I thought it appropriate to put them in this [soprano] clef.]

The way this music was printed did not require all the instruments mentioned
for its performance, nor should the type of figuring, compound or simple, be
taken strictly as an indication of the instrument on which it should be played
(see pp. 29–31).

Many Instruments Accompanying a Single Voice

It quickly became the practice to have many instruments accompanying a
single vocal line; authors encouraged different instruments to play together,
and suggestions begin to appear on appropriate combinations of instruments,
as well as which instruments accompany which voices best. On *chitarrone* and
harpsichords playing together Turini writes:

Ancor che i presenti Madrigali possino esser Concertati con l'Istromento solo da tasto
senza Chitarrone; overo un Chitarrone, ò altro simile Istromento senza quello da tasto;
nulladimeno faranno assai miglior riuscita con l'uno, e con l'altro: poichè l'Istromento

---

[34]   Carlo Milanuzzi, *Primo scherzo delle ariose vaghezze commode da cantarsi a voce
sola nel clavicembalo, chitarrone, arpa doppia, e altro simile stromenti* (Venice, 1622).

[35]   Bartolomeo Barbarino, *Il secondo libro de madrigali de diversi autori per cantare
sopra il chitarrone ò tiorba, clavicembalo, ò altri stromenti da una voce sola* (Venice,
1607).

da tasto non dà quel spirito à i violini che dà il Chitarrone, e il Chitarrone solo senza l'Istromento da tasto riesce troppo vuoto ne li accompagnamenti delle parti di mezzo, e massime nelle ligature, e durezze, e molto più ne le alte; e sonar alla ottava bassa non fa buona riuscita.

Onde à questo effetto si è fatto il presente Basso Continuo duplicato quale serve, non solo per il Chitarrone, ma anco per un Bassetto da Braccio, Viola da gamba, Fagotto, e altri si fatti Istromenti, Concertando tutti bene con i Violini, mà non riuscendo simili sonati continuamente come fa il Chitarrone.

Si avertira di sonarli solamente quando suonano i Violini, e quando sonano, e cantano tutte le parti insieme; il che facilmente si può mettere in essecutione, avertendo alle parole poste sopra questo Basso Continuo, cioè ove dice quando Tutti, e quando Violini, e simili oltre, che serve anco (in caso che non vi sia alcuno de i sudetti Istromenti) per chi regge la battuta potendo facilmente per le medesime sudette parole avisare, e rimettere le parti secondo il bisogno, e conoscere benissimo la natura della Compositione quando vada la battuta spiritosamente, e quando adagio.[36]

[The madrigals presented here may be played with a keyboard instrument alone, without the *chitarrone*; or with a *chitarrone*, or other similar instrument, without the keyboard instrument; nevertheless, they will turn out much better with one and the other: for a keyboard instrument does not give that spirit to the violins which is brought by the *chitarrone*, and the *chitarrone* alone without the keyboard instrument proves too thin in the middle parts – most of all in the *ligature* and *durezze* [dissonances] – and even more in the high range; as to play an octave lower does not turn out well.

Hence to remedy this a duplicated basso continuo part has been given here that can be used not only by the *chitarrone* but by a *bassetto da braccio*, a *viola da gamba*, a bassoon and, as well, other such instruments, all of which go well with the violins but do not have quite the same effect as the *chitarrone* when played throughout.

Make sure to play these instruments only when the violins play, and when all the parts play and sing together; this is easily accomplished by following instructions written above this basso continuo, that is when it says 'Tutti' and 'Violins' and the like; this is useful too (where none of the aforementioned instruments are present) to the person leading the measure [the director] who, with these instructions, can readily take note, distribute parts as needed, and understand well the nature of the composition, when it should be played *spiritosamente*, and when *adagio*.]

Two of the printed part books from Turini's publication are intended for bass instruments; one marked 'Basso continuo per il chitarrone' and the other 'Basso continuo', showing clearly that Turini did expect more than one continuo instrument to be playing these madrigals.

Con che soavità, labbra adorate, from Monteverdi's *Settimo libro de madrigali*, is an exceptional example of an 'orchestrated' madrigal for voice and nine instruments; it illustrates how the continuo section could be best used.[37] The

---

[36] Francesco Turini, *Madrigali à cinque cioè tre voci, e due violini con un basso continuo duplicato per un chitarrone o simil istromento* (Venice, 1629), Libro terzo.

[37] Claudio Monteverdi, *Con che soavità, labbra adorate*, in *Settimo libro de madrigali a 1, 2, 3, 4 e sei voci, con altri generi de canti* (Venice, 1619).

Canto part bears the heading 'Voce Sola che canta con 9 strumenti'; the nine instruments read off separate part-books, and are divided into three 'Chori': the *Primo choro* consists of 'Basso continuo per duoi Chitaroni e Clavecimbalo e Spinetta' (two theorbos, harpsichord and spinet: all plucked instruments, with no sustaining string part). The *Secondo choro* consists of 'Choro di Viole da Braccio a 4, Choro delle Viole all'alta a 4, Viola da Brazzo, Per il Clavecimbano Basso continuo' (four parts for high strings, with the accompaniment of a harpsichord). The *Terzo choro* consists of 'Viola da braccio overo da Gamba, Contrabasso, Basso da Braccio overo da gamba, Basso continuo per l'Organo' (four separate parts for stringed bass instruments, with organ accompaniment).

Monteverdi changes the instruments of the accompaniment according to the words being sung, thus illustrating the text; he assigns the opening *soavità* to the *primo choro*, on *Ma* he changes to the *secondo choro*; with *dolcemente* he joins the *primo* and *secondo choro*; *che soave armonia* is given to the basses of the *terzo choro*; the *O, esclamazione* of *O cari baci* merits the accompaniment of all; and again, at the end, *se foste unitamente* is of course played by all together.

This is an exemplar of what could be done with an ideal number and layout of instruments. Here the inner voices played by the strings are composed not improvised, yet other composers often specified instruments (including melody instruments) without printing any of their parts. Domenico Mazzocchi's madrigal *Passaggio del Mar Rosso*, for example, is marked 'A voce sola, e à 5 accompagnato con le Viole' – but the score is just voice with a continuo line.[38] Most probably, the performers would have written inner parts to be played on the viols, as Monteverdi does; however, only the bass line with figures was printed.

Fabio Costantini's *Ghirlandetta amorosa* has only one part book for the bass, marked 'Basso steso per il cimbalo, overo altri strumenti'. The collection contains five *dialoghi* for three voices marked 'A tre, concertati', yet no indication is given as to how they should be *concertati*, and by whom. The bass part, however, marks clearly which voice is singing so the continuo player knows at all times which character is being accompanied and this is considered enough to indicate how to play appropriately (the same method used by Turini, p. 37); the parts Monteverdi has composed in his work are often left by other composers for the performer to determine.

String Basses Playing in Early Seventeenth-Century Music

Much research has concentrated on defining the role of stringed instruments in the accompaniment of music in the early 1600s,[39] through the study of various documents including frontispieces of printed song collections, accounts of

---

[38]   Domenico Mazzocchi, *Musiche sacre, e morali a una, due e tre voci* (Rome, 1640).

[39]   See, for example, Graham Dixon, 'Continuo scoring in the Early Baroque: the role of bowed-bass instruments', *Chelys*, vol. 15 (1986), pp. 38–53.

individual performances, and musicians' pay-rolls; among the conclusions that have been drawn is that, generally speaking, bowed instruments such as the *viola da gamba* or *violone* were not as common as plucked and keyboard instruments in the accompaniment of vocal music.

Preferences for certain combinations of instruments have been referred to (pp. 36–8); the sound of plucked instruments without a string bass is undoubtedly very special and beautiful, not least for their articulated sonorities, which are covered in the presence of a string bass. The Roman sonatas of Landi and Nicoletti for violin, theorbo and basso continuo, for example,[40] could not possibly be performed with a string bass as the solo theorbo part would be overpowered by the violin together with a string bass in the continuo; the two sonatas *L'Alessandrina* and *La Pazza* of the same collection are specifically scored for theorbo, harp and lute, with no string bass, indicating this was indeed a familiar combination of instruments.

While it seems that string basses were little used in accompaniment where plucked or keyboard instruments were available it must be remembered, however, that composers are the first to ask that the instrumentation be appropriate to the circumstances – taking into consideration the venue, for instance (see p. 43). Records of performances are particular to that performance and choices of instruments and their numbers would have been governed by the circumstances. Certainly there is never any prohibition on whether two types of instruments should play together; it is more likely that all available instruments would have been used to vary the instrumentation as much as possible in accordance with the voices or instruments being accompanied.

There was more need for a string bass in instrumental music than in vocal music; in vocal music the bass line often has a harmonic and supportive role, whereas in instrumental music the bass line can have a melodic function separate from the basso continuo part. There are many examples of bass lines that, from a harmonic accompaniment, suddenly divide onto two staves, thus creating, if only for a few bars, two separate bass lines: a harmonic bass and a diminished bass. In the music of Frescobaldi, as well as others, the Canzonas and Sonatas for soprano and two bass instruments have two separate bass lines, with a clear distinction between the melodic bass line and that used for a harmonic realization; this has been put forward as proof that string basses were only used when a melodic bass line was present as well as the continuo line.[41] Rather it might be the case that a second part-book or second bass line was provided *only* when the bass lines differed. When two bass lines are present, both melodic and harmonic, for long sections the melodic bass often doubles the harmonic bass in any case, suggesting that this was a normal combination to which the ear was accustomed. Throughout the 1600s, and indeed into the following century, instructions are

---

[40]   MS MUS 156 (IRn).

[41]   See Sarah Mangsen, 'The trio sonata in pre-Corellian prints: when does 3 = 4?', *Performance Practice Review*, vol. 3 (1990), pp. 138–64.

written on how to make divisions of the bass as well as on how to simplify a bass line (see Chapter 4).

If the bass line was played by more than one instrument the musicians would have been well aware of their role within the piece, whether they were ornamenting a simple bass line or extracting the main harmonies from a melodic bass line (see pp. 110–12); interestingly, in the later years of the 1600s it became rarer to publish two separate bass lines suggesting that it had become standard practice to adapt the bass line to the instruments being played, rather than implying that now only one instrument was being asked for. The only evidence found that actually warns against certain combinations of instruments playing together is, notably, on the grounds of tuning.

Problems of Tuning

Different temperaments suited certain instruments better than others: according to the theoreticians keyboards played in meantone temperament while fretted instruments preferred to play in equal temperament. The disposition of open strings and frets or the necessary subdivision of an octave on the keyboards were the factors that distinguished different types of instrument.[42]

In 1600 Giovanni Maria Artusi classified instruments into three orders according to their types of tuning. The first order consisted of organ, harpsichord, spinet, clavichord and harps, which worked well together; but lutes, *viole da gamba*, *viole bastarde*, *cetere* and *lironi* were placed in the third order. This is also confirmed in the works of Vincenzo Galilei, Vicentino and Bottrigari. Because of their different systems of tuning, the conclusion was that 'la prima spetie con la terza non può, né potrà mai unirsi senza offesa dell'udito' ['the first kind cannot, and never will be able to play with the third kind without offending the ear']. As early as 1555 Vicentino wrote: 'Mai schiettamente s'accordano quando insieme suonano' ['They are never tuned purely when they play together'].[43] The second 'kind', or order, concerned melody instruments such as cornetts, violins and rebecs. It is not the case, however, that in performance the instruments of the first and third order did not play together. Contemporary documents show how the usual divergence between theoreticians and performers held; while the theorists discussed the impossibilities of tuning harpsichords with lutes and viols, in practice it is clear that, although amply recognized at the time, the disturbance that different tunings caused was not so great as to prevent these instruments from playing together, as the music that was written for them shows; when a harpsichord

---

[42] See Patrizio Barbieri, 'Conflitti di intonazione tra cembalo, liuti e archi nel "concerto" italiano del seicento', in *Studi Corelliani IV, Quaderni della Rivista Italiana di Musicologia* (1986), pp. 123–53 for a more detailed discussion.

[43] Quoted in Mark Lindley, *Lutes, Viols and Temperaments* (Cambridge, 1984), p. 44.

and a theorbo play together in meantone temperament it is more difficult for the theorbo player but the effect is most beautiful to hear.

In 1570 Giovanni de' Bardi wrote to Giulio Caccini: 'piu fiate mi è venuto voglia di ridere, videndo strafelare i Musici per bene unire viola, o liuto con istrumento di tasti ... fino a questo giorno non anno avvertita cosa di tanta importanza, e se avvertita, non rimediata' ['more than once I have wanted to laugh, seeing musicians tiring themselves out to unite a *viola* or lute with a keyboard instrument ... until now it was never felt to be anything of much importance; or if it was felt, it was never remedied'].[44]

The instruments Cavalieri recommends, specifying that the effect of their ensemble is particularly beautiful, would have been forbidden under these tuning orders: 'una Lira doppia, un Clavicembalo, un Chitarone, ò Tiorba che si dica, insieme fanno buonissimo effetto: come ancora un Organo suave con un Chitarrone' ['a *Lira doppia*, a harpsichord, a *chitarrone* or theorbo (however one wants to call it) together sound very well indeed, as do a sweet organ with a *chitarrone*].[45]

It is Doni who states that the way musicians hid what he calls 'dissonances' – that is, problems with incompatible tuning – was to make divisions: 'quelli, che suonano il Liuto, o Tiorba con gli Organi, o Clavicembali, sempre diminuiscono; perchè se usassero botte piene, vi si conoscerebbe la dissonanza' ['those that play lute or theorbo together with organs or harpsichords always make diminutions because if they played full chords, one would hear the dissonance'].[46]

Barbieri, accepting Doni's explanation for divisions being played, suggests the style of lute playing Agazzari is attacking here is also due to tuning problems between instruments:

Onde chi sona leuto, essendo strumento nobilissimo fra gl'altri, deve nobilmente suonarlo con molta inventione, e diversità; non come fanno alcuni, i quali per haver buona dispostezza di mano, non fanno altro che tirare, e diminuire dal principio al fine, e massime in compagnia d'altri stromenti, che fanno il simile, dove non si sente altro che zuppa, e confusione, cosa dispiacevole, et ingrata, à chi ascolta.[47]

[Therefore those who play the lute, being one of the most noble instruments, must play it nobly with much invention and diversity; unlike some who, just because they have good dexterity in the hand, do nothing but runs and diminutions from beginning to end, especially when in the company of other instruments, who do the same, and then you can hear nothing but soupiness and confusion, which is most unpleasant and thankless for those listening.]

---

[44] Quoted in Lindley, *Lutes, Viols and Temperaments*, p. 44.
[45] Cavalieri, *Rappresentazione di Anima, et di Corpo*.
[46] Doni, *Trattato della musica scenica*, in *De' trattati di musica*, II, p. 111.
[47] Barbieri, 'Conflitti d'intonazione'.

A more likely reason for this kind of diminution on the part of continuo players was to keep the sound of their instruments alive – an essential technique of plucked instruments and harpsichords.

It is unquestionably difficult for fretted and keyboard instruments to tune together in the more extreme meantone temperaments; no attempt will be made here to give a solution as to how this should be done; in performance it is the ears of the musicians that must react and adapt to each tuning (as they would have done in the 1600s) while avoiding the 'soupiness and confusion' that is the result of failing to listen to others carefully and respond co-operatively.

In any case, the difficulties of massed continuo playing lay elsewhere:

Le fatiche poi, i disgusti, gli affanni, e i rammarichi, che i poveri Musici provano in aggiustare insieme tanti Sonatori, e suoni in un luogo così angusto, appena si crederebbono; perchè con molto perdimento di tempo, e confusione bisogna disporre gl'Istrumenti, e distribuirne i lumi, collocare i sedili, rizzare i leggii, e accordare gl'Istrumenti: e Dio sa se dopo averli bene accordati, bisogna di tutto spesso rifarsi da capo per la moltiplicità delle corde, e rallentamento loro per rispetto de' lumi, e quanto bene si possano raggiustare, mentre gli altri suonano: senza parlare della fatica, e del tempo, che si mette in fare tante copie dell'intavolatura del Basso, e di altri disordini, che seguono da questa miscellanea, senza alcun fondamento introdotta.[48]

[The pains, the distastefulness, the anxieties and the sorrows that the poor musicians feel in arranging together so many players and sounds in so narrow a place, would scarcely be believed. For, with much loss of time and confusion, they must arrange the instruments, distribute the lamps, order the seats, set up the music stands, and tune the instruments. And God knows if, after tuning them well, they don't often have to do the whole thing again from the beginning, because of the multiplicity of the strings and their slackening on account of [the heat of] the lamps, as well as they can be readjusted while the others are playing. To say nothing of the trouble and time it takes to make so many copies of the *intavolatura* of the bass, and of other problems which result from this miscellany, introduced without any grounds.]

Basso Continuo Performance in Larger Works

Explicit indications in the introductions to solo song books, as well as the notation used for the accompaniment, indicate that more than one instrument could be playing even if just one voice was singing. The desire to hear a more substantial bass line with many instruments realizing the bass in different ways was a taste developed in theatrical pieces; in part because of the need to fill a larger volume of space with sound, more instruments played. *Melodramma* uses the continuo for expressive purposes, enhancing and responding to the *affetti* expressed in the singing; most importantly, basso continuo shed its role as a simple, harmonic support and now played an active part in the success of the drama. Basso continuo

---

[48]   Doni, *Trattato della musica scenica*, in *De' trattati di musica*, II, p. 110–11.

in larger works is now considered as a group of instruments playing as an entity – instruments used for accompaniment are employed for dynamics and colour, and descriptions of continuo performances in large-scale works discuss in what combinations these instruments should play and when, as well as how they can best accompany in order to respond to the vocal part in the most effective way.

Alessandro Guidotti, printer of Emilio de' Cavalieri's *Rappresentazione*, writes: 'Gli strumenti siano ben suonati, e più, e meno in numero secondo il luogo, o sia Teatro, overo Sala ... Et il Signor Emilio laudarebbe mutare stromenti conforme all'affetto del recitante' ['Instruments shall be well played, varying in number according to the venue, be it a theatre or a large room ... And Signor Emilio is very much in favour of changing instruments in accordance with the *affetto* of the singer'].[49]

In this manner continuo instruments reinforced the effects the singers created. Of the first work for larger forces, Pietro de' Bardi writes: 'La prima poesia, che in istile rappresentativo fosse cantata in palco, fu la Favola di Daphne del Signor Ottavio Rinuccini, messa in musica dal Peri ... Fu cantata sopra un corpo di strumenti' ['The first poem to be sung on stage in *stile rappresentativo* was the fable of Daphne by Ottavio Rinuccini, set to music by Peri ... It was sung over a body of instruments'].[50]

Considerable discernment is needed to think how the instruments of this *corpo di strumenti* might have been used; while there are many accounts which are very precise in giving details of other performances, listing instruments employed, their numbers and, at times, even the names of the performers, it should be noted that the instrumental balance was a sensitive issue of the utmost importance to the composers; a common piece of advice found in these descriptions, as in the Cavalieri, is that the number of instruments should depend on the size of the venue and their role within the work, for example if they were on or off stage; players' lists are indicative only of the physical circumstances for a particular performance and of the choice of forces the composer made.

It is certain, however, that large numbers of instruments were encouraged, offering the possibility of maximum variety in the accompaniment; Doni writes:

Nell'azioni cantate dove mi son trovato qui in Roma, e in Firenze, ho veduto quasi indifferentemente adoprare ogni sorte d'istrumento più nobile, clavicembali, viole, tiorbe, liuti, lire e che so io? ma in particolare i clavicembali di forma grande; avendosi per opinione che senza essi non si possa fare perfetta armonia; attesochè vi si trova ogni sorte di consonanze e si suonano comodamente con l'esempio innanzi, e finalmente perchè oggi regnano assai; anzi mi pare che gli odierni musici, come il sig. Emilio del Cavaliere nella sua *Rappresentazione* e il sig. Claudio Monteverde nel suo *Orfeo*,

---

[49] Cavalieri, *Rappresentazione di Anima, et di Corpo*, Preface.

[50] Pietro de' Bardi, *Lettera a G.B. Doni sull'origine del melodramma* reproduced in Angelo Solerti, *Le origini del melodramma*, p. 146.

diano per consiglio di mettere in essa quasi ogni sorte di questi istrumenti e in gran numero.[51]

[In the musical dramas which I attended here in Rome, and in Florence, I saw every sort of noble instrument employed almost without distinction, harpsichords, *viole*, theorbos, lutes, *lire* and who knows what else? but particularly the larger harpsichords, the prevalent opinion being that perfect harmony cannot be attained without them, since any kind of consonances may be found in them and they can be comfortably played with the example [score] in front of one, and finally because nowadays they are most fashionable; indeed, it seems to me that contemporary musicians, such as Emilio del Cavaliere in his *Rappresentazione* and Claudio Monteverde in the *Orfeo*, recommend that almost any type of these instruments be used, and, moreover, that a great number of them be employed.]

While confirming the common use of large forces of diverse instruments in these grand works Doni notes that sometimes particular instruments – the large harpsichords – are favoured. Certain combinations were used more frequently than others and, in the works for smaller forces, each voice or instrument was accompanied by its own continuo instrument; in the case of larger works a whole continuo section could be allocated to an individual character.

Monteverdi describes clearly how each character in his *Tirsi e Clori*[52] should be accompanied by their own continuo section:

giudicherei per bene che fosse concertato in mezza luna, su li angoli de la quale fosse posto un chitarrone e un clavicembano per banda, sonando il basso l'uno a Clori e l'altro a Tirsi, e che anch'essi avessero un chitarone in mano, sonandolo e cantando loro medesimi nel suo e li detti duoi istrumenti (se vi fosse un'arpa in loco del chitarone a Clori, sarebbe anco meglio); e gionti al tempo del ballo, dopo dialogati che averanno insieme, giongere al ballo sei altre voci, otto viole da braccio, un contrabbasso, una spinetta arpata (se vi fossero anco duoi leuttini piccioli, sarebbe bene).[53]

[I would judge this piece to be played best in a half moon shape at the corners [outer edges] of which a *chitarrone* and a harpsichord per group should be placed, one playing the bass for Clori and the other for Tirsi; they too should hold their own *chitarrone*, playing it and singing their own part along with the two instruments mentioned (a harp instead of a *chitarrone* for Clori would be even better); and once they come to the dance, after they have had their dialogue together, another six voices should be added to the dance, eight *viole da braccio*, a double bass, a *spinetta arpata* (if there were also two little lutes that would be good).]

---

[51]   Doni, *Trattato della musica scenica*, in *De' trattati di musica*, II, p. 104.
[52]   Monteverdi, 'Tirsi e Clori', *Settimo libro de madrigali*.
[53]   Claudio Monteverdi, *Lettere* to Annibale Iberti, 21 November 1615, ed. Domenico De' Paoli (Rome, 1973).

Monteverdi chose plucked instruments to accompany voices, and string basses to play with violins in the instrumental sections, as well as during the choruses, where plucked and bowed instruments are both present; his careful choices seem to have escaped Doni's ear (pp. 43–4).

Precise details for instrumentation are given in the printed score of *L'Orfeo* of 1609.[54] Being a printed edition it served a commemorative function rather than being the performing score; a consideration of the instruments listed, however, and their use in the opera, makes an interesting study for even if in performance the instruments did not play exactly as specified, Monteverdi nonetheless has left a paradigm of how the instruments can be used.[55]

The continuo instruments listed in *L'Orfeo* are: 'Duoi Gravicembali, duoi contrabassi de Viola, dieci Viole da brazzo, un Arpa doppia, duoi Chitaroni, duoi Organi di legno, tre bassi da gamba, quattro Tromboni, un regali' ['Two harpsichords, two *contrabassi de viola*, ten *viole da braccio*, an *arpa doppia*, two *chitarroni*, two wooden organs [i.e. with wooden pipes], three *bassi da gamba*, four trombones, a regal']. Throughout the score Monteverdi annotates in what combinations these instruments should play, and where; they way he groups the instruments characterizes each dramatic situation.

Monteverdi uses different continuo groups for individual singers in the dialogue between the Pastore and Messaggera: the Pastore is accompanied by a harpsichord, theorbo and a *viola da braccio*, Messaggera by one organ and theorbo.

It is the sonorities of the instruments that characterize the normal world and the underworld; the *Coro de spirti* of the underworld sings to the sounds of regal, organ, five trombones, two bass *viole da gamba*, and a double bass. At the end of the act the underworld instruments cease, and the more usual continuo instruments return to play: 'Taccion li Cornetti, Tromboni e Regali, e entrano a sonare il presente Ritornello, le viole da braccio, Organi, Clavicembani, contrabasso, e Arpe, e Chitaroni, e Ceteroni, e si muta la Sena' ['Cornetti, trombones and regals cease playing, and for this *Ritornello* the *viole da braccio*, organs, harpsichords, doublebass, harps, *chitarroni*, and *ceteroni*, should enter, and the scene changes'].

This distinction between the instruments of the underworld and those of the normal world remains even when accompanying one voice: in the third act, Caronte sings to the regal alone, whereas in *Possente spirto* Orfeo is accompanied by an organ and a theorbo, typically one of the most beautiful combinations for accompanying voices; to cross the Styx, he sings accompanied by just an organ, for greater intimacy.

---

[54] Claudio Monteverdi, *L'Orfeo, favola in musica* (Venice, 1609).

[55] Indeed, as Paolo Fabbri points out in *Monteverdi* (Turin, 1985), p. 114, there are inaccuracies in the printed score; the instruments listed at the beginning of the opera are fewer than those called for during the course of the work.

In the fifth act, Monteverdi calls for two continuo groups made up of the same instruments, organ and theorbo. These should be situated on either side of the stage as the scene involves voices *in echo*; in this way, each continuo group can be nearest the singer it is accompanying on stage.

In the fourth act there is a beautiful illustration of the changing of instruments according to the *affetti* being sung. Orfeo, accompanied by harpsichord, *viola da braccio* and theorbo sings:

> Ma che odo oimè lasso?
> S'arman forse à miei danni
> Con tal furor le furie innamorate,
> Per rapirmi il mio bene, ed io 'l consento?

He turns to Euridice and to the accompaniment of organ alone sings:

> O dolcissimi lumi io pur vi veggio,
> Io pur:

But he is to lose her forever and, returning to the previous continuo sound of harpsichord, *viola da braccio basso* and theorbo, sings:

> ma qual Eclissi ohimè v'oscura?

Monteverdi makes changes in instrumental sonority as Cavalieri says, 'mutare stromenti conforme all'affetto del recitante', even for just two bars, according to the *affetto* of the moment – exactly what he was doing with the bass instruments in *Con che soavità* (discussed on pp. 37–8). Such precise annotation of sonorities enables basso continuo performers today to create appropriate accompaniment perhaps more than the list of players, descriptions of placings, or accounts of instruments and numbers of instruments.

Indications in Other Operas

L'Orfeo is extraordinary because of the indications for instrumentation printed in the score, not just because of the way the instruments are used. The detail with which the instruments are orchestrated by Monteverdi is in sharp contrast to the usual practice in *melodrammi*; many instruments are expected to play but rarely are indications given on the score as to how they should act, leaving the orchestration up to the performers; in Michelangelo Rossi's *Erminia sul Giordano*, there is simply the indication *Basso continuo per tutti gli strumenti* at the beginning of the opera, with no other indications for the continuo in the remaining three acts.[56] Stefano Landi, in his *Il S. Alessio*, gives two bass lines, almost identical, the first marked *Arpe, Leuti, Tiorbe e Violoni*, the second marked *Basso continuo*

---

[56]   Michelangelo Rossi, *Erminia sul Giordano* (Rome, 1637).

per Gravicembali; on very few occasions does he specify which group should play in preference to the other, and he never divides the two groups (for example, combining a harpsichord with a *violone*).[57] In performance, however, because it is so undesiderable to limit possible instrumental combinations in this way it is likely that there were as many instrumental changes as those marked in *L'Orfeo*; it is rare for printed scores to note these changes.

Contemporary descriptions of how pieces could be orchestrated that do exist, as in *L'Orfeo*, taken with the reasons outlined here as to why they should be so orchestrated, offer some guidance for performance today.

The Accompaniment of Instrumental Music

There are many more accounts of the accompaniment of vocal music from the first half of the 1600s than of instrumental music; the style was new, still exciting attention and amply commented upon. Music was subordinate to text, and the *affetti* of the text were reflected in the composition and expressed in performance; instrumental music had no text to follow yet this manner of writing had become so imbued in the style of composition that this embodiment of *affetti* in composition and its reflection in performance was not specific to vocal music alone.[58]

Frescobaldi's famous introduction to the first book of Toccate of 1615 notes: 'Nel progresso s'attenda alla distintione dei passi, portandoli più e meno stretti conforme la differenza de i loro effetti, che sonando appariscono' ['In the development [of the piece] take care over the distinction [separation] of passages, make them more or less driven, in compliance to the difference of their effects [*affetti*] that appear while playing'].[59]

He says, and it is evident in his music, that *affetti* are written into his work and should be portrayed in performance. In the reprint which appeared a year later he further expands and explains how vocal *affetti* influence instrumental music: 'Primeriamente; che non dee questo modo di suonare stare soggetto à battuta; come veggiamo usarsi ne i Madrigali moderni, i quali quantunque difficili si agevolano per mezzo della battuta portandola hor languida, hor veloce, e sostenendola etiandio in aria, secondo i loro affetti, ò senso delle parole' ['First, this way of playing should not be subject to the beat, as we see in modern madrigals, which regardless of their difficulty, are assisted by their use of the beat making it now languid, now quick, suspending it in the air according to the *affetti*, or sense of the words'].

---

57   Stefano Landi, *Il S. Alessio* (Rome, 1634).

58   An extended commentary on the relationship between vocal and instrumental music in the 1600s is given by Andrea dell'Antonio, 'La maniera di cantare con affetti cantabili: the seconda prattica and instrumental music' in *Syntax, Form and Genre in Sonatas and Canzonas 1621–1635* (Lucca, 1997).

59   Girolamo Frescobaldi, *Primo libro di toccate e partite d'intavolatura di cimbalo* (Rome, 1615), Al lettore.

As the same principles as those for vocal performances can be applied to the execution of purely instrumental music, the *nuovo stile* of composition having become common to both, changes in the instrumentation of the continuo apply also when accompanying instruments, and should be sensitive enough to reflect changes in the *affetti* of the musical text.

The notation of instrumental music Instrumental music was often printed in score – if instruments were missing for a performance it was expected that their parts would be included in the realization of the basso continuo; whereas if all the voices were available an actual basso continuo realization could be dispensed with.
Lorenzo Allegri writes:

> Hò voluto situare le Sinfonie spartite per commodità dell'Istrumenti perfetti come Liuto, Organo, e in particulare dell'Arpa doppia. Si possono sonare co 'l primo Soprano, e con due Soprani, e 'l Basso continuato, inmanchanza [sic] dell'altre parti; oltre con Viole, e Istrumenti di fiato co 'l Basso continuato e senza.[60]

> [I have put these *Sinfonie* in score for the sake of perfect instruments such as the lute, the organ and especially the *arpa doppia*. They may be played with the first soprano, and with two sopranos and the basso continuo, in the absence of the other parts; they can also be played with *viole* and wind instruments with or without the basso continuo.]

Often the requirements were simply that there be a soprano line and a bass, and the middle parts were left to the interpretation of the performer. Keyboard music could be adapted for many instruments just as instrumental music could be performed on a keyboard alone; it was common for the keyboard repertoire of the period to be printed on four staves, in open score.
Often explicit indications for the distribution of the parts on different instruments appear in keyboard publications. Gregorio Strozzi's *Capricci da sonare cembali et organi* is printed in score;[61] despite the title of the publication, other instruments appear in small print at the beginning of some of the pieces. In particular, the *Romanesca con partite* requires that the 'Parte Undecima' be played by 'Arpa, Viola, ecc.'; the *Gagliarda terza* is marked 'per concerto di viole'.
Frescobaldi's *Primo libro delle canzoni* is printed in open score. Grassi, the publisher, discusses the reasons for this choice: 'Hò posto questo volume in partitura accio sia comodo à i professori d'ogni sorte di strumenti, e che nell'istesso tempo possino vedere tutte le parti cosa necessarissima à chi desidera sonar bene. Ogni Sonatore potrà sonare queste Canzoni in compagnia, e solo' ['I have set this volume in *partitura* so that it may be useful to practitioners of every sort of instrument, who will be able to see all the parts at the same time – a most necessary

---

[60] Lorenzo Allegri, *Il primo libro delle musiche* (Venice, 1618).
[61] Gregorio Strozzi, *Capricci da sonare cembali et organi* (Naples, 1687).

feature for those who wish to play well. Every player will be able to play these Canzoni with others and alone'].[62]

In this particular publication, both *partitura* and separate part books exist. Grassi then writes that the first book of *Toccate* – which had been printed on two staves – presented difficulties as new scores had to be made for performance on anything other than keyboard, showing that this was an already established practice.

> Il Primo Libro delle Toccate del medesimo Signor Girolamo, che è stato a i virtuosi di grandissimo gusto per non essere in partitura, è stato necessario à chi hà voluto servirsene per altri stromenti di accomodarlo con gran fatica alla loro intavolatura onde posso sperare che tanto più deve esser gradita quest'opera mentre ognuno può accomodarvi sopra qualsivoglia sorte di stromento.[63]

> [[In] the First Book of Toccatas by the same Signor Girolamo, which has been much treasured by every virtuoso for not being in *partitura*, it was necessary for those wishing to use it with other instruments to adjust it with much hardship to their *intavolatura*; I hope, therefore, that this work shall be even better received, because anyone can adjust it to any kind of instrument.]

The intabulation of instrumental music allowed for these two interpretations: either a keyboard instrument playing from four staves, or four different instruments playing one stave each. If these different instruments were all harmony instruments, then each of the four parts would consist of the written part and its own harmonization.

Sacred Music and Basso Continuo

Problems of Notation

Some composers and theoreticians initially brought out strong arguments against the introduction of basso continuo as the only means of notating the accompaniment. The major criticism of basso continuo as its use became widespread was that, because of the purely harmonic nature of the notation, organists were no longer taking care over their counterpoint; church musicians were determined in opposing, at least theoretically, the introduction of basso continuo in sacred music. Adriano Banchieri laments that because of this new harmonic accompaniment organists had become lazy, and underqualified people who were not musically prepared to accompany contrapuntally in the old manner

---

[62] Girolamo Frescobaldi, *Il primo libro delle canzoni a una, due, tre, e quattro voci* (Rome, 1628).

[63] Frescobaldi, *Il primo libro delle canzoni a una, due, tre, e quattro voci*, 'Alli studiosi dell'opera'.

of the previous century, were nonetheless able to accompany successfully using
basso continuo, 'calling themselves organists':

> Questo nuovo modo di suonare sopra il Basso non lo biasmo, ma non lodo però che gli
> novelli organisti tralascino di studiare le ricercate a Quattro voci, e fantasie d'huomini
> Illustri nella professione, atteso, che oggidi molti con quattro sparpagliate di mano, e
> suonare sopra un Basso continuo si tengono sicuri Organisti, ma vero non è atteso che
> sicuri Organisti sono quelli i quali suonano un ben tirato Contraponto che si sentino
> tutte quattro le parti.[64]

> [I do not criticize this new way of playing the bass, however nor do I praise it as young
> organists neglect to study the *ricercate* for four voices, and the *fantasie* of reputable
> men in our profession; nowadays many [organists] just by sprawling about a bit with
> their hands and playing from a basso continuo regard themselves as fine organists, but
> this is not true as competent organists are those who play a well-drawn counterpoint
> so that all four parts can be heard.]

While deploring the fact that organists have stopped studying the works of the
great masters, as one of its inventors Banchieri cannot wholly condemn this 'nuovo
modo di suonare il basso', this new way of playing the bass; he acknowledges
the advantages and greater practicality for the new compositions of playing from
a basso continuo part but perhaps does not want its superficial ease of use to
supplant the musical knowledge and training upon which its best use relies.

There can be no excellence in performance in basso continuo accompaniment
without a thorough knowledge of counterpoint; to depart knowledgeably from the
rules is very different from unwittingly breaking them. That a system responding to
the need for flexibility and expressiveness has also yielded a way to avoid learning
an organist's skills can only be regarded as a deleterious side effect.

His concerns about the drawbacks of basso continuo led him to be one of the
initiators of the practice of *Partimenti* (discussed fully on pp. 76–9). Here a bass
line with figures is given, above which the skilled contrapuntalist must compose. It
is not specifically an exercise in basso continuo realization, but it does require and
enhance the skills of improvising on a bass line and reconciles the new practice
of basso continuo figures with the older contrapuntal teaching.

Taking a more favourable viewpoint on basso continuo, Agazzari states at the
beginning of his *Del sonare sopra 'l basso* (1607) that the musician 'deve saper
suonar bene il suo strumento, intendendo l'intavolatura, ò spartitura' ['must know
how to play his instrument well, and understand *intavolatura*, or *spartitura*'], but
ends the treatise arguing for the superiority of the figured bass: 'non è necessario
far spartitura, ò intavolatura; ma basta un Basso con i suoi segni, come abbiamo
detto sopra' ['it is not necessary to do a *spartitura* or *intavolatura*; a bass with its
signs [figures], as explained above, will suffice'].

---

[64] Adriano Banchieri, *Dialogo musicale* in *L'organo suonarino* (Venice, 1611), p. 11.

It should be noted that he assumes a capability to write out a *spartitura* or *intavolatura*. It is the very nature of basso continuo that is at the heart of Banchieri and Agazzari's differing opinions, for it is a type of accompaniment that is purposefully moving away from the idea of playing each voice of an open score, in order to give the performer greater flexibility; also Banchieri is referring specifically to organists whereas Agazzari is more concerned with basso continuo realization on all instruments.

Agazzari also considers the *intavolatura* the least clear system of notation. Even if it were possible to intabulate all the melodic lines the hands cannot play them all note for note, especially when there are many parts. The result, he writes, is a score in which the individual contrapuntal lines cannot be followed through, nor is it possible to simplify the part to only the harmonies as the *intavolatura* is too confusing to follow. Agazzari concludes by saying that the *intavolatura* actually holds back the organist from playing anything other than the written notes whereas he believes the organist's role to be no longer merely to support the singing parts but to add to the ensemble with improvisations where appropriate.

Agazzari provides one of the clearest presentations of the view that accompaniment even in sacred music needed to be liberated from a system of notation that did not allow the flexibility required by the new style of composing; he writes, 'conchiudendo non esser bisogno, ne necessario à chi suona, far sentir le parti come stanno, mentre si suona per cantarvisi, e non per sonar l'opera come sta, che è diversa cosa dal nostro soggetto' ['[I] conclude that there is no need, nor is it necessary for the player to make the parts heard as they are, as one plays so as to be sung to, not to play the work as it stands, which is something different from our topic'].

Accompaniment on the Organ

The introductory comments found in printed collections for the use of organists also suggest that composers and publishers sometimes found it difficult to reconcile the requirements of the music (and of printing), which called for the accompaniment to be written in basso continuo, with the skills of the organists who might find themselves in difficulty if faced with anything other than an *intavolatura*. That organists relied heavily on the *intavolatura* is apparent from the reaction of the composers when accompaniment began to be printed as basso continuo.

Rognoni states that the *partitura* is best: 'alcuni amici m'hanno detto che questa opera ordinariamente sarà suonata, e che vi fà bisogno del Partito; onde per compiacerli l'ho dato fuori, conoscendo che in ogni caso meglio è il Partito, che il Basso continuato' ['some friends told me that this work will be played often, and so there will be a need for a *partitura*, so to please them I have done this, knowing that in any case a *partitura* is better than a *basso continuato*'].[65]

---

[65] Domenico Rognoni, *Canzoni à 4 e 8 voci* (Milan, 1605), Partito.

Massaini distinguishes between good and bad continuo players, warning of the damaging effects an inadequate realization can have on the whole piece: 'se ben tal volta hò udito alcun suonatore, che habbia suonato à proposito con questi Bassi continuati, ne hò pero udito infiniti, che con il loro suonare pieno di mende affatto, levano alle compositioni l'aria, e l'essere, che gli ha dato il proprio Padre' ['Although occasionally I have heard a player who has performed well from these bassi continuati, I have also heard a great many who, with their playing entirely full of flaws, deprive the compositions of the grace and being that their author gave them'].[66]

He adds that *intavolature* were for musicians less experienced playing from a figured bass; as a guide for the continuo player he prints one of the upper voices above the bass: 'Io havea pensato di stampar seco l'Intavolatura per maggior commodità di semplici suonatori, e Monache, ma hò mutato pensiero per non accrescere tanto il Volume, che però hò posti appresso al Basso, una parte che sempre canti ... ' ['I had thought of printing with this the *intavolatura* for the greater ease of simple players, and nuns, but I changed my mind so as not to increase the Volume too much, however I have placed, above the bass, a part that is always singing ...'].

Despite resistance on the part of the organists a basso continuo part was becoming the most common system of notation; organists were told that if they 'lacked the art of music' and could not read basso continuo they were to make their own *intavolatura*: 'Finalmente sarà bene, che quelli Organisti, che non sono pratichi a sonar sopra il Basso seguito, e che non possiedono l'Arte della Musica, volendo haver sodisfattione di questa sorte di concerti, li spartino, e l'intavolino' ['Finally, it is best that those organists who have no experience in playing from a *Basso seguito*, and who do not possess the Art of Music, wishing to be pleased by these kinds of *concerti*, should make scores of them, and *intavolature*'].[67]

Merula, writing in 1615, almost ten years after these publications, suggests for the first time that organists might actually prefer to play from a continuo part; it is quite possible that organists' skills had changed and adapted to the times; nonetheless, as did Banchieri, he continues to frown upon the practice: 'Benche per maggior facilità di li Signori Organisti vi sia posto il Basso continuo alle presente Canzoni laudo nondimeno il partirle' ['Although, for the greater ease of the organists, there is a basso continuo part for these Canzoni, nonetheless I approve of [making] a *partitura*'].[68]

Publishers who were quick to pick up on the organists' unfamiliarity with basso continuo notation began to supply *intavolature* to works issued without.

---

[66]   Tiburtio Massaini, *Musica per cantare con l'organo ad una, due e tre voci* (Venice, 1607), Partitura.

[67]   Giovanni Piccioni, *Concerti ecclesiastici ... a una, a due, a tre, a quattro, a cinque, a sei, a sette, e a otto voci, con il suo basso seguito per l'organo* (Venice, 1610).

[68]   Tarquinio Merula, *Il primo libro delle canzoni a quattro voci per sonare con ogni sorte di stromenti musicali* (Venice, 1615).

The Venetian publisher Vincenti wrote out *intavolature* himself for other people's compositions: 'Aspettate honorati Virtuosi da me continuamente nove inventioni per facilitarvi la strada alle fatiche con Intavolatura, Passaggi, e Partidura: delle quali già ne hò fatte alquante sorte, e ne andrò facendo, come vegga che voi ve ne serviate, e che vi sia grata l'opera mia' ['Expect from me, honoured *virtuosi*, ever new inventions to ease your laboured way with *intavolatura, passaggi* [ornaments] and scores [*partitura*]: of which I have made already various kinds, and shall make more, as long as I see that you make use of them, and find my work of value'].[69]

In 1602 he published Ludovico Grossi da Viadana's *Cento Concerti Ecclesiastici*; in the *Avvertimenti* are contained one of the first sets of instructions on continuo playing, which take up some of its most important issues. The instructions are numbered:

> Secondo. Che l'Organista sia in obligo di suonar semplicemente la Partitura, e in particolare con la man di sotto, e se pure vuol fare qualche movimento dalla mano di sopra, come fiorire le Cadenze, ò qualche Passaggio à proposito, ha da suonare in maniera tale, che il cantore, ò cantori non vengano coperti ò confusi dal troppo movimento.

> [Second. The organist is obliged to play only the score, particularly with the lower hand [that is, the left hand], and if he should wish to make some movement with the upper hand, such as embellishing cadences, or some appropriate passages, he must play in such a way that the singer, or singers are not covered or confused by too much movement.]

This severe instruction that the left hand must be played as written is followed by the admonition that right-hand flourishes, even at cadences, should be done discreetly.

'Quarto. Sia avvertito l'Organista di far sempre le candenze ai lochi loro' ['Fourth. The organist should always play cadences in their place']. He goes on to explain that when accompanying a soprano voice the realization at cadence points should be in the soprano range; similarly, when accompanying a tenor the realization must be in the tenor range. He stresses that it would be most undesirable to play in the tenor range when accompanying a soprano, or in the soprano range when accompanying a tenor. Viadana is freeing the organist from doubling the sung parts but he is also giving a warning to stay nontheless in the range of the voice that is singing. This is an indication often repeated in other publications; the vocal line was becoming more ornate and therefore it was not desirable to double it exactly. It is from this organ tradition that the style of the doubling of cadence formulas in their exact register derived (discussed pp. 119–21).

---

[69]   Imogen Horsley, 'Full and short scores in the accompaniment of Italian church music in the early Baroque', *Journal of the American Musicological Society*, vol. 30 (1977): pp. 466–99.

'Quinto. Che quando si trovarà un Concerto, che incominci à modo di fuga l'Organista, anch'egli cominci con un Tasto solo, e nell'entrar che faranno le parti sij in suo arbitrio l'accompagnarle come le piacerà' ['Fifth. When the organist finds a concerto that begins in a fugal manner, he too should begin *tasto solo*, and as the other parts enter he will judge best how to accompany them as he pleases'].

As well as confirming that fugal entries should be doubled, this rule underlines the organist's licence to accompany according to taste once all the parts have entered, no longer being obliged by the *intavolatura* to carry on doubling the parts as written.

> Sesto. Che non si è fatta la Intavolatura à questi Concerti, per fuggir la fatica, ma per rendere più facile il suonargli à gl'Organisti, stando che non tutti suonarebbero all'improviso la Intavolatura, e la maggior parte suonaranno la Partitura, per essere più spedita: però potranno gl'Organisti à sua posta farsi detta Intavolatura, che a dirne il vero parla molto meglio.

> [Sixth. No *intavolatura* of these concerti has been made, not to escape the work, but to render their playing easier for organists, as not everybody can sight-read an *intavolatura*, and most of them play from a *partitura*, as it is quicker; yet organists may still make an *Intavolatura* themselves, which to tell the truth is much better.]

Viadana confirms one of the main advantages of basso continuo to be the facility with which it can be sight read, as Agazzari had pointed out in his second reason to praise basso continuo (quoted on p. 22).

Relinquishing counterpoint Viadana's ninth *Avvertimento* concerns parallel fifths and octaves: 'Nono. Che non sarà mai in obligo la Partitura guardarsi da due quinte, nè da due ottave; ma sì bene le parti che si cantano con le voci.' This has been translated in various ways (it is deliberately left in the original here). Tagliavini reports that a Latin translation of Viadana's *Cento Concerti* published by Nicolaus Stein in Frankfurt (1609, 1613, 1620, 1626) suggests that it means the doubling of the sung parts is to be avoided.[70] Praetorius has a different interpretation; he interprets the verb *guardarsi* as meaning *being careful* rather than *avoid*, therefore saying that the organist should pay attention to the vocal parts rather than being careful about any parallel fifths or octaves that might occur in the accompaniment. Haack interprets it as meaning that the organist must avoid fifths and octaves between the instrumental accompaniment and the vocal parts; but this cannot be right because it does not coincide with the practices of the time, which allowed these almost unavoidable parallel octaves between instrumental parts and the singing parts; it would also be a contradiction of Viadana's twelfth *avvertimento*,

---

[70] Luigi Ferdinando Tagliavini, 'Review of Helmut Haack, Anfänge des Generalbaßsatzes. Die "Cento Concerti Ecclesiastici" (1602) von Lodovico Viadana (Tutzing, Hans Schneider 1974)', *Rivista Italiana di Musicologia*, 13 (1978): pp. 174–85.

where the octave doubling of the voices at cadences is not only allowed, but recommended as it provides beauty and grace (*vaghezza*).

The correct interpretation, as Tagliavini establishes, is that Viadana wishes to stress that the ban on parallel fifths and octaves does not apply to the *accompagnamenti* the organist is playing; it applies to the composed vocal parts which still have to obey the rules of correct voice-leading, whereas the role of the accompanist is to execute the correct *concordanze* – that is, consonances. That this passage should be misinterpreted at the time it was written, as well as today, suggests not only that the concepts it describes were new then, but also that today it is still difficult to accept that the rules of counterpoint are not and never were rigidly applicable to basso continuo in Italy. The Italian school of continuo playing is based on this distinction: a thorough knowledge of counterpoint was required to form the background from which continuo players were gradually allowed to depart, following other sets of rules.

Certainly the importance of counterpoint in composition was not diminished by the rise in popularity of basso continuo, but that Viadana, the first chronicler on continuo playing, should stress in 1602 that parallel fifths and octaves are allowed by the style confirms that the distinction between composition and basso continuo accompaniment is already in place. By 1614, even Banchieri tells the organist not to worry about parallel octaves between the accompaniment and the part which is singing. However, it still took almost twenty years before *intavolature* ceased to be published in connection with this style of music, despite Viadana's teachings, which are the most comprehensive of all his contemporaries. Viadana's music is innovative in that the bass, together with whatever number of parts he writes, needs to be filled in harmonically, yet the result is not contrapuntal but a true accompaniment in the new style.

Using the score without doubling the parts Vocal pieces written in the new *concertato* style contain indications to the organist on how to accompany virtuoso singing; the soprano line is provided although sources are clear that the vocal part is not to be doubled note for note on the organ:

> Con la Partitura poi dell'Organo, appresso il Basso continuo, con gli accidenti soliti segnati, si è posta anche la Parte piu accuta; non perche l'organista l'habbi a rappresentare continuamente, ma si bene a fine, che havendola innanzi a gli occhi possa e aiutare e discretamente accompagnare il cantante, massime quando resta solo, accio gli sia per mezzo di tal discretezza e accentare e con passaggi di suo gusto dar quella perfettione che gli parerà esser conveniente a tal concerto.[71]

> [As for the organ score, above the basso continuo, with the usual accidentals marked, the highest voice has also been included; this is not for the organist to represent continuously [that is, double it throughout], but so that, having it before his eyes, he

---

[71] Girolamo Giacobbi, *Prima parte dei salmi concertati a due, e più chori* (Venice, 1609).

might help and discreetly accompany the singer, especially when he remains alone, so that by means of such discretion he shall accentuate and, with *passaggi* of his liking, give that perfection which he judges most apt to the ensemble.]

Giovanni Paolo Cima writes:

Mi favoriranno anco li valenti Organisti quando soneranno questi (solo con Basso, e Soprano) accompagnarli con le parti in mezo con quella maggior diligenza che sia possibile, perchè gli accompagnamenti grati fan grato il Canto … Et scuoprendo passi alquanto licenziosi; considerino le parole, overo l'effetto della Musica, che troveranno esser fatta ogni cosa con sano giuditio. Et benche nel Partito in molti luoghi ci siano le gratie, come stanno nelle parti; l'ho fatto acciò si vegga lo stile; oltreche anco è di molto agiuto al Cantore suonargli talvolta l'ornamento. Ma per lo più giudicarei essere bene, toccare solo il fermo, rimettendomi però del tutto al perfettissimo giudicio loro.[72]

[Great organists will do me the favour, when they play these [pieces] (with just the bass and soprano), to accompany them with the middle parts as diligently as possible, for pleasing accompaniments make the singing pleasing … And in discovering somewhat daring passages, may they give due consideration to the words, that is the *affetti* of the music, and they will find that everything has been done with sound judgement. And although in the score in many places there are graces, as there are in the parts, I did this so that the style might be seen; as it is sometimes of great help to the singer to play him the ornament. But mostly I should judge best to play only held notes, relying, however, completely on [the organist's] own most perfect judgement.]

Organists were still being given the *partitura* but were now asked, indeed told, not to treat it as an *intavolatura*, thereby playing the parts as written, but to play chords from the bass line using the voice parts as a stylistic guide, allowing the singer freedom during the ornamented passages.

Ercole Porta writes:

… servendosi anco il saggio Organista dell'orecchio, per non haver in molti luoghi (massime nella Messa) segnato intieramente le consonanze, e disonanze, e ciò per non offuscare i poco pratici sonando anco con poco numero di consonanze, nel ristretto d'una, e due voci, riserbandosi porre in opera, e mani, e piedi, ne i ripieni senza però aggiunta di registri; ben che di ciò non occorra avisare i prudenti di tal arte.[73]

[… for the wise organist must also avail himself of his ear, as in many places (particularly in the Mass) I have not marked the consonances and dissonances, in order not to confound the inexperienced when a limited number of consonances is required in the accompaniment of one or two voices, while hands and feet must be put to work in the

---

[72] Giovanni Paolo Cima, *Concerti ecclesiastici, à una, due, tre, quattro voci* (Milan, 1610).

[73] Ercole Porta, *Sacro convito musicale … a una, due, tre, quattro, cinque, e sei voci* (Venice, 1620).

ripieni, without however adding registers; although, of course, sensible players hardly need to be reminded of this.]

His instruction to play more or fewer notes according to how many voices are singing is a rare indication of how basso continuo was used, allowing a response to the parts that were being accompanied: few notes should be played when only one or two voices are singing, and the greater volume needed in the ripieno sections should be achieved by playing fuller chords, with the possible addition of pedals, rather than by adding registers.

Banchieri is cautious in his use of registration but suggests its use to increase volume: 'In concerto deve assestarsi sicuro nella battuta, sonar grave ne offuscare con tirate e grillerie gl'affetti e passaggi del Cantore posti nelle Cantilene; servirsi con giudizio nel ponere gli Registri alla quantità e qualità delle voci' ['When playing with others [the organist] must establish the beat securely, play low and not cover with runs and ornaments the *affetti* and *passaggi* of the singer written in the vocal part; he must use his good taste regarding registration according to the quantity and quality of the voices'].[74]

This is not merely an indication to play elegantly and with good taste; it is a sure indication that the organ should be played in such a way as to respond fully to the type of voice accompanied, although in this case adding or removing registers according to however many parts are singing.

Other types of notation   There were two further types of scores associated particularly with the accompaniment of church music on the organ: the first presents, in score, the lowest voices of each of the choirs in a polychoral work. The second is a short score where either the soprano and the bass are given (highest and lowest parts of a composition), or a three-voiced short score is given as a reduction of six or more voices onto three lines.[75]

Appropriateness of Use in these Systems of Notation

A consideration of the *Bassus generalis* part of a most celebrated work, Monteverdi's *Vespri della Beata Vergine* of 1610,[76] sees all these types of printed accompaniment employed, according to the complexity and delicacy of the movement accompanied. The movements are scored as follows:

1   *Domine ad adiuvandum*: the bass line together with the first voice part is given.

---

[74]   Adriano Banchieri, *Dialogo musicale* in *L'organo suonarino* (Venice, 1611), p. 11.

[75]   See Horsley, 'Full and short scores in the accompaniment of Italian church music' for more details on these forms of notation.

[76]   Claudio Monteverdi, *Sanctissimae Virgini Missa Senis Vocibus* (Venice, 1610), Bassus Generalis.

2   *Dixit Dominus*, sex vocibus e sex intrumentis: the bass line alone is given; this is sufficient and economical as there would be twelve separate voices to print for the voices to be represented fully.

3   *Nigra sum*, motetto ad una voce: the bass and vocal part are given, aiding the organist in the accompaniment of a most complex vocal part.

4   *Laudate pueri*, à otto voci sole nel Organo: 3 staves are printed. The lowest part is the bass line; the middle part outlines fugal entries; the top part represents the highest voice at any given point. This works well as the singers have the note for each of their entries and the organist reads off three staves rather than nine. When the solo section begins at bar 15, the ornamented vocal parts are given in full – an example of what Cima was saying, that the organist is only expected to play the long held notes, not the fast passages (which are there as a guide). On these three staves is all the information needed for performance, and the organist's judgement should be used as the occasion dictates; the organist can prompt as the voices are represented, yet the printing of a full score has been avoided.

5   *Pulchra es*, a due voci: the bass line with both voices is given in full – indeed, quite exceptionally, here the voice parts are printed with more ornamentation than in their own part book.

6   *Laetatus sum*, a sei voci: as *Laudate pueri*, on three staves.

7   *Duo Seraphim*, tribus vocibus: the bass line and three voices are given complete throughout.

8   *Nisi Dominus*, a dieci voci: the voices are too many and the writing too complex to distil onto two or three staves; here only the bass line is given.

9   *Audi coelem*, sex vocibus: at the beginning the bass line and the tenor part are given; when the other voices enter no vocal line remains, leaving only the unfigured bass part, with the exception of the tenor flourishes in bars 67–69 and 88–92.

10 *Lauda Jerusalem*, a sette voci: just the bass line is given, with no figures; as in the *Nisi Dominus*.

11 *Sonata sopra Santa Maria ora pro nobis*, à otto: just the bass line is given except in bars 19–33 and 41–45 where the violins duet; here a simplified version of the violin parts is given. In the other movements none of the vocal parts given is ever simplified – it is evident that the organist is not expected to play the vocal, ornamented part, which is there only as a guide; in this case, however, it is probable that the organist was intended to play, if not both violin parts, at least the lowest throughout this solo. Unfortunately this has been misrepresented both in modern editions and in performance, often leaving no accompaniment – although doubling one of the parts, or even both as Monteverdi's notation implies should be done, sounds very good.

12 *Ave maris stella*, hymnus à otto: only the bass line is given.

13 *Magnificat*, septem vocibus, e sex instrumentis: just the bass line is printed, but registration indications are given, adding a register at each entry of the voice.

- *Et exultavit* a tre voci, only the bass line is given. As the bass moves in minims it is hard to know where to place the second note – hence the specification 'va sonato tardo perchè li doi tenori cantano di semicroma' ['this must be played slowly as the two tenors are singing semiquavers'].
- *Quia respexit*, just bass line is given, warning the organist that the instruments will be loud; indications on when the accompaniment should be loud and when it should be soft are given by the registration markings *Principale, ottava, e quintadecima* alternated with *principale solo*.
- *Quia fecit*, again, makes sense of the warning 'si suona adaggio perche le parti cantano e sonano di Croma et Semicroma' ['play this slowly as the parts are singing and playing quavers and semiquavers'], as only the bass line is given, moving in semibreves.

For a continuo player the publication is ideal; all the essential information is given concisely. In the movements where many instruments and many voices are employed only the bass line is given, and none of the upper parts; there is no need for the upper parts to be represented, as there are no delicate moments to accompany where the organist must be aware what the voices are doing. Where only the bass is given the organist is expected to play the harmony implied by the bass line. In the movements with only continuo accompaniment, without instrumental parts, a short score is used as a way to mark the many, difficult fugal entries. This allows the organist to be sure that the voices are entering correctly and, by playing their parts, that the singers are singing the right notes. Of course the organist can play chordally at any point and abandon the three staves, using them simply as a guide to what the other parts are doing. In the solo motets the ornamented vocal lines are given in full, with their complete ornamentation, so that the organist might sensitively accompany the voice although it is not intended that the vocal part should be doubled. In the Magnificat the only two movements in open score are the most complex for the upper parts, both with voices in echo. It is the difficulty of accompanying, rather than the complexity of the upper parts, that dictates the type of score that was printed for each movement.

To guide the accompaniment in this composition Monteverdi has drawn upon a variety of notations, each fitted to the number of voices and the ornateness of the solo writing, the whole being enclosed in a single work. He uses the notation to illustrate the style in which he wishes the accompaniment to be performed, showing how his organist must have competence in both the 'old style' *intavolatura* as well as in the more responsive basso continuo; both styles of compostion and performance continued to be practised.

The long-lasting effect *intavolatura* had on accompaniment style both in sacred and secular music was the practice of doubling the solo line, despite the accompaniment being read from a basso continuo part or from a *partitura* with improvisation above the bass line guided by the parts. While generally thought of today as something to avoid, it is clear that from the earliest days of basso continuo at the beginning of the 1600s until quite late in the seventeenth century this practice was widespread and, indeed, often specifically recommended (pp. 119–21). In sacred music, the practice persisted despite the change in notation, and specific requests to stop doubling any highly ornamented vocal line had to be made.

Breaks with the contrapuntal tradition of the previous century were not clearly defined but there developed a separation of the concept of continuo playing from the contrapuntal approach necessary in composition. The further the continuo player was encouraged to depart from the score and from the rules of counterpoint, the more necessary it became to dispel harmonic doubts and establish matters of style; too much detail was being left to the *buon gusto* of the players; rules had to be drawn up to delineate these matters of style in order to teach the following generation of keyboard players more precisely what this *buon gusto* involved. In what follows attention is focused on the rules and indications offered to keyboard players and, more specifically, to harpsichordists.

Chapter 4

The Eighteenth Century

Le regole d'accompagnamento – Rules of Accompaniment in the Eighteenth Century

Commonly continuo players performed from an unfigured bass; by the end of the seventeenth century, often not even the part that was being accompanied was included. The need to guide performers in their harmonic and stylistic choices resulted in the *regole d'accompagnamento*, which begin to appear at the beginning of the eighteenth century. These are a specific set of rules that explain where, rhythmically, chords should be placed according to the movement of the bass, and instructions on how unfigured basses should be harmonized.

These rules of accompaniment, much referred to in sources of the time, are most fully expounded in print by Geminiano Sangiovanni in his *Primi ammaestramenti della musica figurata*,[1] a detailed and comprehensive treatise with much emphasis on practical issues. Francesco Gasparini too sets out these rules of accompaniment in Chapter IV of his *L'armonico pratico al cimbalo*,[2] but the rules are not labelled or separately considered as such; they fall under the chapter heading 'Osservazioni sopra i moti per salire, e prima di grado'. While some parts of Sangiovanni are taken almost word for word from Gasparini's *L'armonico pratico*, which might explain the lesser fame of Sangiovanni's treatise, the rules of accompaniment are presented there in a particularly clear manner.

In manuscript form the *regole* can be determined from three main sources. Alessandro Scarlatti teaches the *regole*, entitling them *Per accompagnare il cembalo, ò organo, ò altro stromento*.[3] Various, and slightly differing, copies of the manuscript survive, showing how widespread was his teaching.[4] The *Regole accompagnar sopra la Parte N.1 d'autore incerto*,[5] an anonymous manuscript hereafter referred to as Roma N.1, is another main source. The *regole* are also

---

[1]   Geminiano Sangiovanni, *Primi ammaestramenti della musica figurata* (Modena, 1714).

[2]   Francesco Gasparini, *L'armonico pratico al cimbalo* (Venice, 1708).

[3]   Alessandro Scarlatti, *Per accompagnare il cembalo, ò organo, ò altro stromento* (GBLbl, Add. 14244).

[4]   For a discussion of the manuscript see Tagliavini's Introduction to the Forni facsimile edition. Here, GBLbl, Add.14244 has been used.

[5]   *Regole accompagnar sopra la Parte N.1 d'autore incerto* (IRli, MS Musica R. 1).

discussed in anonymous manuscripts on basso continuo held in the Museo internazionale e Biblioteca della musica di Bologna.[6]

Precisely because so much Italian music is not figured, or is only partially figured, a knowledge of these rules is vital and their application in performance is essential. Performers today have even greater need to practise ways of harmonizing this music than had musicians wholly familiar with the musical sounds and conventions of the time; that within the *regole* is explained both the placing of chords within the bar and the harmonies expected to be heard when only an unfigured bass is given makes the *regole* one of the most important sources of stylistic information available.

The *regole d'accompagnamento* refer to a chordal accompaniment; they are not general rules for the accompaniment of the voice or instrument, rather they are general rules for the accompaniment of the bass line itself. Already a very specific approach to basso continuo is apparent; the skill lies in knowing how to accompany the left-hand bass line, rather than being concerned about the manner of accompaniment of another part (see p. 123 for how this skill developed). Its method of teaching is that used throughout the eighteenth century, giving the roots above which divisions and ornaments can be played (pp. 87–112), yet even performing according to the the *regole* alone results in a strong and beautiful style of accompaniment. Here, the clearest examples are taken from all these sources to give a complete overview of this style of playing.

The level of teaching in these sources is by no means aimed at beginners; figures given as exemplary harmonizations quite early in the treatises involve sevenths and ninths to be prepared and resolved correctly, and the exercises found at the end of some of the treatises, to be realized according to the *regole*, are very difficult. None of the exercises, in any of these sources, is realized. An editorial realization has been avoided here as well, as the explanations on where, rhythmically, chords should be placed are perfectly clear; the most effective way to understand these practical exercises is to try them at the keyboard realizing each example according to the instructions.

Rhythm

In 4/4 The first rule is layed down most clearly by Gasparini. In 4/4, when there are four crotchets ascending by step, the first crotchet takes a full chord, and the following three should be accompanied lightly, with just a third.

> si potrà suonar piena la prima, e nell'altre farà buonissimo effetto tenendo fermo il Tasto, che fà l'Ottava con la prima nota, accompagnarle tutte con la Terza, o Decima. Ma con un sospiro avanti si suonino tutte piene, dando la sesta naturale alle due di mezzo.

---

[6]   IBc Mss E.25, K.22, K.36, K.81, P. 120, P. 132, P. 134, P. 138, P. 140.

[the first [crotchet] takes a full chord, and in the others it will sound well to hold the key that forms the octave with the first [bass] note, and accompany them all with a third or a tenth. However, when there is a rest at the beginning they should all take a chord, the two middle notes taking a major sixth.]

By contrast, when there is a rest at the beginnning of the bar the following three crotchets all take a chord, while the rest does not take a chord (Example 4.1[7]).

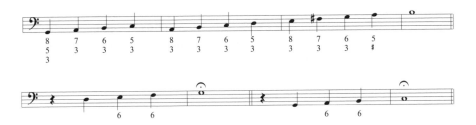

Example 4.1   F. Gasparini, *L'armonico pratico*, p. 34

With quavers Sangiovanni states that ascending and descending quavers should be accompanied by a chord on each crotchet so that the first quaver is strong and the second weak: 'e si considera la prima per buona, e l'altra per cattiva' ['the first is considered good, and the second bad']. The concept of strong and weak notes is fundamental in performance – in basso continuo the number of notes in each chord is weighted so as to reflect this accentuation within the bar. This particular rule is one of the few practical guidelines printed in the first books on continuo; Francesco Bianciardi is one of the many authors who explains how this effect can be achieved (Agazzari, Sabbatini and other, minor, authors also confirm this rule).[8] In his *Breve regola per imparar' a sonare sopra il basso* Bianciardi states:

> Quando il Basso procede per note diminuite, ò per tirate; si fa la consonanza sopra alla prima nota della battuta, in modo che delle tirata ne venga una buona, e una gattiva. Cosi quando ci sarà la minima, e seminima col punto, si fa la consonanza sovra il punto, e la nota, che segue, passa per cattiva.

> [When the bass proceeds by diminished notes, or scales, the consonance is placed on the first note of the bar, so that in the scale there is a good and a bad note. Thus when there is a minim, and a dotted crotchet, the consonance is played on the dot, and the following note is bad.]

---

[7]   The page numbers in the example captions refer to the 1704 edition.

[8]   Francesco Bianciardi, *Breve regola per imparar' a sonare sopra il basso* (Siena, 1607); Agostino Agazzari, *Del sonare sopra 'l basso con tutti li stromenti* (Siena, 1607); Galeazzo Sabbatini, *Regola facile e bene per sonare sopra il basso continuo nell'organo, manacordo, o altro simile stromento* (Venice, 1628).

Gasparini too writes that the chord should be placed every two quavers, stressing the good but not the bad notes; in practice this rule is an indication that when the bass moves by step, the second of two quavers is to be treated as a passing note and should not be harmonized. Bismantova phrases it well when he states: 'Il tempo in aria, che è il 2° ò 4° della Battuta alle volte non si considera, andando di Grado' ['The beat in the air, that is the second or fourth of the bar, is sometimes not considered, when moving by step'].[9]

However, as Sangiovanni points out, it is also possible to play a chord on each quaver (Example 4.2), making as much harmony as possible – a general stylistic point he takes this opportunity to emphasize: 'Suonando nel Cembalo, le Crome benchè di grado, si potranno accompagnare tutte, o quasi tutte, acciocchè si renda maggiore, e più grata armonia' ['Playing the harpsichord, quavers moving by step can all be accompanied, or nearly all, in order to obtain a greater and more pleasing harmony'].

Example 4.2   G. Sangiovanni, *Primi ammaestramenti, Esempio 20*, p. 24

In Example 4.2, while it is not necessary for each quaver to take a new harmony (for example, the fourth and eighth quaver of the first bar do not need to be harmonized), this is certainly an excellent exercise, as Sangiovanni says, for realizing the bass in the fullest way, both for the number of chords and because of the addition of sevenths and other dissonances.

Semiquavers should be accompanied four at a time whether ascending or descending, as in Example 4.3. Four semiquavers are allowed to pass under one harmony and the chord is reiterated at each crotchet. However when, as in Example 4.4, semiquavers move by leap, a chord should be played with every quaver. Although the harmony does not change on every quaver, Sangiovanni requests a chord for effect rather than of necessity, as such movement in the bass line calls for a vigorous accompaniment.

Example 4.3   G. Sangiovanni, *Primi ammaestramenti, Esempio 21*, p. 24

---

[9]   Bartolomeo Bismantova, *Compendio musicale* (Ferrara, 1677), p. 76.

Example 4.4   G. Sangiovanni, *Primi ammaestramenti, Esempio 22*, p. 24

In performance, the number of chords in the right hand depends also on the tempo of the piece; Alessandro Scarlatti's *regole* seem generally to apply to a quicker tempo than that of the other authors. He writes that when the bass moves in crotchets, the first should be accompanied but not the second ('una buona, e l'altra cattiva'), a treatment the other authors reserve for quavers; when the bass moves in quavers, Scarlatti advises placing a chord every four notes ('una buona, e l'altre tre cattive'), as the other authors write for semiquavers. In Example 4.5, a chord should be given on the first quaver and the following three should pass without a chord. When the bass moves by leap every note should be accompanied both in crotchets and quavers (Example 4.6). Here, as in Example 4.2, the harmony does not require a different chord on each note, though to do so renders the accompaniment pleasingly rich.

Example 4.5   A. Scarlatti, GBLbl, Add.14244, folio 5

Example 4.6   A. Scarlatti, GBLbl, Add.14244, folio 5

Sangiovanni explains that when there is a quaver leap at the beginning of the bar the three quavers that follow all take a chord (Example 4.7). However, he gives an example of quavers to be accompanied in pairs (Example 4.8; such a sequence of suspensions is more melodic than the figurations used in the previous examples). When quavers move by leaps, it is nearly always the case that each quaver should be accompanied as should the quaver that ends the leap, even if then it moves by step (Example 4.9).

Example 4.7   G. Sangiovanni, *Primi ammaestramenti, Esempio 17*, p. 24

Example 4.8   G. Sangiovanni, *Primi ammaestramenti, Esempio 18*, p. 24

Example 4.9   G. Sangiovanni, *Primi ammaestramenti, Esempio 19*, p. 24

Having dealt with the most common bass lines the continuo player is likely to encounter, the *regole* then treat more delicate matters of style.

Rests and cross-accentuation A rest on a strong beat, for example at the beginning of a bar, can be accompanied in two ways: by placing a chord on the rest, or not placing a chord on the rest – both are strong in effect.

Sangiovanni states that when there is a quaver rest followed by three quavers all three notes should be accompanied by the right hand; the implication is that a chord should not be placed on the rest (Example 4.10). The advantage of such an accompaniment is that it allows the performer to change the emphasis within the bar by accentuating the second beat, which normally should be weak. Similarly, chords can be used to displace the accentuation within the bar. In a piece in 3/4 where the bass moves as in Example 4.11, instead of a chord being placed every two notes it can be restruck on the third quaver, forming tension with the upper parts that remain in 3/4.

Example 4.10   G. Sangiovanni, *Primi ammaestramenti, Esempio 16*, p. 24

Example 4.11   A. Vivaldi, Concerto for *flautino* and strings in C major, RV 433, Allegro, opening bars

Examples of the opposite, that is placing a chord on the rest, are found in connection with the accompaniment of semiquavers. Tonelli's realizations of Corelli's opus V provide such an example in the ninth variation of *La Follia* (Example 4.12);[10] in the first half of the variation chords are placed on the first and second beats of the bar when the bass line has a rest on the second beat; Tonelli could well have chosen to respect the rest and to place the chords on the first and third beats but does not do so. In the second half of the variation, however, the bass line's rest has moved to the third beat but the right hand has also changed, with chords on the first and third beats, again not respecting the rest, never allowing a rest in both hands at the same time; a rest in the bass line does not equal silence.

In the treatises distinctions are made between how to accompany semiquaver rests and quaver rests. On accompanying semiquavers, Sangiovanni writes: 'Nel tempo di ciascun sedicesimo si battono prima le Consonanze, o sia l'accompagnamento della prima Semicroma con la mano destra, e poi con la sinistra si passano le altre tre' ['When playing in semiquavers you should first play the consonances, that is the accompaniment of the first semiquaver, with the right hand, then with the left hand let the other three [semiquavers] pass'] (Example 4.13).

Alessandro Scarlatti, in his *Toccata per cembalo d'ottava stesa*, exemplifies this rule (Example 4.14). One of the anonymous Bologna manuscripts states that a chord should be given on the rest, whether in quavers or semiquavers:

> Si deve poi osservare, che nel sonare il basso continuo si trovano certi andamenti spezzati, che invece della nota, vi è una pausa, e questo è negl'andamenti di Crome, e semicrome ... si batte con la mano di sopra l'accompagnamento che porta quell'andamento nel tempo che passa il valore di detta pausa.[11]

> [Note that while playing basso continuo some 'broken movements' are found where, instead of the note, there is a rest; this happens with quavers and semiquavers ...

---

[10]   Antonio Tonelli, *Della quint'opra d'Arcangiol Corelli / Basso per tasto d'Antonio Tonelli* (IMOe, Mus. F1174). Tonelli provides a written-out accompaniment for the whole of Corelli's Opus V; these realizations exemplify many of the practices described in treatises of the time, unlike Alessandro Scarlatti (p. 81), and invite careful study – yet their limitation is, as with all written-out realizations, that by their annotation they cease to be improvisatory, and the performer is subject to the decisions on appropriateness and taste of the author (p. 79).

[11]   *Regole per il basso* (IBc, P. 134, folio 97v).

Example 4.12   A. Corelli/A. Tonelli, *La Follia*

[6]

Example 4.13   G. Sangiovanni, *Primi ammaestramenti, Esempio 23,* **p. 25**

Presto

Example 4.14   A. Scarlatti, *Toccata per cembalo d'ottava stesa*

the upper hand should play the accompaniment in the time of the movement which corresponds to the value of the rest.]

This anonymous author encourages a chord to be placed on the rest both with quaver and with semiquaver movements.

Both treatises and musical examples concur in expecting a chord at the beginning of the bar when the bass is quick (a semiquaver rest followed by three semiquavers). Vivaldi's *Suonata à violino, oboè, et organo obbligato* RV 779 (Example 4.15) bears the indication 'Si accompania solamente la prima nota del batter, e levar' ['only accompany the first note of the downbeat, and of the upbeat']. This means a chord should be given on the first beat of the bar leaving the scale to run without harmonization and, most importantly, without reiterating the chord on the top note, that is the second beat of the bar. A chord should then be placed on the second half of beat two (the upbeat to the half-bar) and then again on on beat three, as the figuration is repeated. By following Vivaldi's simple indication the organist adds a further distinctive rhythm to the composed parts; a chord was expected on the demisemiquaver rest in order to give impetus to the upbeat.

Both solutions to how a rest should be accompanied (putting a chord on the rest, or avoiding putting a chord on the rest and moving it to somewhere else in the bar) are explained in the *regole*; the conclusion that can be drawn is that when the bass moves slowly in crotchets or quavers the rest should not be accompanied with a chord, but with a faster movement in semiquavers a chord should be given over the rest. In practice, what should be borne in mind in placing the chord is the effect the chord will have – it can stabilize the beat when it falls on the rest at the beginning of the bar when moving in semiquavers, as in Example 4.12, which is particularly useful when playing together with other bass instruments; or, in its opposite function, disturb the ensemble by playing off the beat, creating the

Example 4.15   **A. Vivaldi, *Suonata à violino, oboè, et organo obbligato*, RV 779, Saxon State and University Library (Mus. 2389-Q-14)**

same effect as accentuating every third quaver in a 3/4 piece, effectively forming an extended hemiola.

Sangiovanni recommends that a dotted note or syncopated rhythm in the bass should nonetheless be accompanied by placing chords in order to stabilize the bar.

> Quando il Basso fa Nota puntata, e che essa Nota fia di Valore qualche poco lungo, si ribatteranno gli accompagnamenti di mezzo, quali si sono dati ad essa Nota a proporzione del Valore del Punto ... Il medemo si fa ancora nelle Note di una battuta, o mezza, o fia di due quarti, o sincope, compartendo meglio il Valore di essa Nota per poter meglio andare a tempo giusto, e a battuta perfetta.[12]

> [When the bass plays a dotted note, and this note is quite long, the middle accompaniments should be restruck in proportion to the value of the dot ... The same should be done with notes that last a beat, or half a beat, that is two crotchets, or syncopated notes, [thus] dividing the value of the note well in order to be able to play in time better, and with a perfect beat.]

The right hand was often called upon to play in this chordal, simple manner when the compositional writing risked unsettling the ensemble.

Triple time Sangiovanni explains that 'Nelle Triple o di Minime, o di Semiminime, ovvero di Crome, quando vanno di grado, per lo più si accompagna la prima Nota del battere, e la terza, che va nel levare della battuta' ['In triple time with mimims, crotchets or quavers, when they move by step, mostly the first note of the downbeat is accompanied, as well as the third, which is the upbeat of the [following] bar']. In Example 4.16 the first and third notes of the bar both take a chord; the instruction from Gasparini, however, is to accompany only the downbeat, and the effect is very different. Certainly Sangiovanni's suggestion, as in the previous examples, results in a very rich style of accompaniment.

---

[12]   Sangiovanni, *Primi ammaestramenti della musica figurata*, p. 34.

Example 4.16   G. Sangiovanni, *Primi ammaestramenti, Esempio 24,* **p. 25**

The same should be observed in 6/4 and 6/8 (Example 4.17), and in 12/8 the accompaniment should fall every three notes (Example 4.18).

Example 4.17   G. Sangiovanni, *Primi ammaestramenti, Esempio 25,* **p. 25**

Example 4.18   G. Sangiovanni, *Primi ammaestramenti, Esempio 26,* **p. 25**

All rhythmic possibilities are now covered, but with a word of warning from Gasparini that while to play punctiliously in this manner is good for beginners, expert players should use their judgement as to which are the most appropriate accompaniments: 'essendo così più facilità per i Principianti, mentre il Pratico poi opararà con giudicio, e distinzione de' tempi, e degl'andamenti' ['like this it is easier for beginners, whereas the Expert will operate with judgement, distinguishing *tempi* and pacing'].

Having set out when and where to place a chord according to the type of movement of the bass the *regole* then concentrate on the harmonization of an unfigured bass line.

Adding Notes to the Harmony

Basic harmonic principles and the harmonization of unfigured yet straightforward bass lines are commonly dealt with first in most sources, with exercises; examples of the most commonly found bass lines are given, and their most simple harmonization explained. These examples are not illustrated here; it is relatively straightforward to harmonize an Italian eighteenth-century unfigured bass, although the harmonization is ultimately dependent on the composer's score (as composers in the 1600s were pointing out, see p. 25).

Alessandro Scarlatti says: 'Altre regole universali non ponno darsi, perchè il modo di componere moderno hà escluse molte regole antiche, per l'inventione dell'uso moderno della modulazione, ò sia tessitura dell'armonia' ['Other universal rules cannot be given, for the modern way of composing has excluded many old rules, because of the variety in the modern use of modulation, or range of the harmony'].[13]

Tonelli advises always playing from the score in order not to make mistakes, and to accompany in the most appropriate manner: 'Ma il più nobil Consiglio, che in tal maniera dar si possa è l'uso del suonare in Partitura, poichè da quella s'ottiene la guida più certa, e sicura d'un più fino, e valido Accompagnamento' ['But the best advice that can be given in this way is to acquire the habit of playing in *partitura* [score], from which the most accurate and reliable guide for a fine and valid accompaniment is obtained'].[14]

Sangiovanni agrees, stating that the most reliable way to be sure of playing the right harmonies is to read the part that is being accompanied together with the bass: the organist must read the part he is accompanying, as 'the notes ... serve as numbers'.

> Di più nelle Composizioni a Voce sola l'Organista deve essere assai pronto, e con l' occhio, e orecchio attento al Cantante, massime quando vi è collocata di sopra la Parte, che canta, perchè (non essendovi li Numeri sopra il Basso, o almeno pochi, come ancora pochissimi ♯♯, o ♭♭ molli) allora le Note di detta Parte, che canta, fanno l'uffizio delli Numeri.[15]

> [Particularly in compositions for solo voice, the organist must be very alert, and aware of the singer with his eyes and ears, especially when their part is placed above the bass line because (if there are no numbers above the bass, or there are only a few, and yet fewer sharps or flats) then the notes of the part that is singing serve as numbers.]

Eighteenth-century Italian compositional style is concentrated principally in the writing for voice or violin or, in orchestral pieces, in the writing for strings; it has been noted that the harmonic structure is often simple and any counterpoint in the upper voices of the score was expected to be reduced to harmonic blocks in the continuo realization. The difficulty for the continuo player, freed from the rules of counterpoint (p. 54), is to learn to add dissonances and suspensions to the 'correct', simple harmonies implied by the bass alone. The *regole* explain what to do and the circumstances in which it was desirable to add these extra notes to the harmony.

Alessandro Scarlatti's written rules support harmonically rich playing:

> È da notare per bella maniera di sonare (e questo è secondo lo stile di chi scrive in questo libro) tutte le volte che accade la consonanza di sesta maggiore, si aggiunge la 4.a sopra la 3.a di detta consonanza, perchè fa bel sentire.

---

[13] Scarlatti, *Per accompagnare il cembalo* (GBLbl, Add.14244), p. 40.
[14] Antonio Tonelli, *Teorica musicale ordinata alla moderna pratica* (IBc, MS L. 54), folio 36v.
[15] Sangiovanni, *Primi ammaestramenti della musica figurata*, p. 35.

[Note that to play beautifully (following the present writer's style) whenever there is a consonance of a major sixth, the fourth should be added to the third of this consonance, for it is pleasing to hear.]

A simple $^6_3$ chord should therefore be performed as a $^6_4{}^3$ chord; this was a contested issue, however, as Gasparini writes that the fourth is acceptable only as an *acciaccatura*, and it is not until Manfredini, as late as 1775, that the fourth is discussed as an integral part of the harmony.[16]

Again, Scarlatti writes:

> Da notarsi, che similmente per modo grato di sonare, tutte le volte che si fanno cadenze, ò pure movimento del basso di 4.a in sù, o 5.a in giù, alla 3.a maggiore della nota del basso, che è per moversi in detta maniera, vi si aggiunge la 7.a minore, perchè fa buon sentire.

> [Note that, again in order to obtain a pleasing style of playing, every time there is a cadence, or the bass moves up a fourth, or down a fifth, to the major third of the bass note which is moving in such a manner, one adds a minor seventh, because to hear it is beautiful.]

At cadence points then, a seventh must be added.

Giovanni Paisiello gives a formula regarding ninths: 'ascendendo di 3a si aggiunge la 9a' ['when [the bass] rises by a third, the ninth is added'] (Example 4.19).[17] He adds that, as a general rule, the ninth should be accompanied with the tenth and the second, conceding that these do not always need to be prepared – indeed, in Example 4.19 it is impossible to correctly prepare and resolve all the dissonances, particularly as these are doubled (see pp. 82–3).

Example 4.19   G. Paisiello, *Regole per bene accompagnare il partimento, o sia il basso fondamentale*

Ornamentation too was expected in the realization of the bass line; *acciaccature* formed an integral part of the chord – however, they are taught separately, after the harmonic *regole* have been mastered; here they are considered from p. 87.

---

[16]   Luigi Ferdinando Tagliavini, personal communication.

[17]   Giovanni Paisiello, *Regole per bene accompagnare il partimento, o sia il basso fondamentale* (INc, MS 33-2-3).

Sangiovanni gives examples of when the rules need not be observed: 'Quando ad una Nota sono segnati li Numeri, non si fa Regola alcuna, come le soprascritte, ma si accompagna quella Nota, come dicono li Numeri' ['When numbers are placed beneath a note, the rules described above are not observed, and the note is accompanied in accordance with the numbers'].[18] That is, when there are figures these should be played even if they are surprising and against the general harmonic rules for the accompaniment of an unfigured bass.

'Quando una Nota sarà di poco valore, e a quella se li dovrebbero dare varj accompagnamenti uno dopo l'altro, (come nelle Regole soprascritte) in detto caso se li darà un'accompagnamento solo' ['In the case of a short note that should be given the accompaniments as described in the *regole* above one after the other, only one accompaniment should be given'].[19] Sangiovanni means there may not always be time to play all the harmonies required by the *regole* – for example, at a cadence point it is not always possible to play a $\frac{5}{3} - \frac{6}{4} - \frac{5}{4} - \frac{5}{3}$ formula on a minim – in these cases, the harmonization should be simplified.

Harmonization of scales Sangiovanni closes the section on harmony with an example of an extremely luscious harmonization of a G major scale, remarkable for its use of suspensions, sevenths and ninths, upward resolutions and having two harmonies per chord (Example 4.20).

10	9 8	10		9 8	7 6♮	6	5		5 6	6 6	6♯	6	6 6	10	10	
9 8	7 6	9 8		7 6	5 8	5	4	3	3 4♯	3 4	3 4	♯ 4♯	3 4♯	7 6	8	
5 6♯	5♯ 10	5 6		5 ♯	3				2	2	2♯	2	2	5♯ 8	7 6♯	

Example 4.20   G. Sangiovanni, *Primi ammaestramenti, Esempio di Note di grado in sù, e in giù con false risolute in arpeggio continuo*, p. 28

This harmonization is all the more striking when put in the context of scale harmonizations of the time. Many of the harmonizations found in the anonymous treatises consist simply of 5–6 progressions ascending and 7–6 progressions descending, not harmonizations in the modern sense of the word. Stradella[20] gives two examples of a G major scale. One is of the 5–6, 7–6 variety (Example 4.21), but the other (Example 4.22) is a more extravagant harmonization; here, alternative figurings are given, one above and one below the bass line.

---

[18]   Sangiovanni, *Primi ammaestramenti della musica figurata*, p. 34.
[19]   Sangiovanni, *Primi ammaestramenti della musica figurata*, p. 34.
[20]   MS attributed to Stradella, *Regole* (IBc, P. 120), pp. 33–6.

Example 4.21   IBc, P. 120, ms attributed to Stradella, *Regole*, pp. 33–6

Example 4.22   IBc, P. 120, ms attributed to Stradella, *Regole*, pp. 33–6

Stradella also gives an interesting realization of a scale (Example 4.23); in the left hand, the chords are often made of the fifth and the octave, a chordal spacing that is found in the solo repertoire for harpsichord of the previous century. The number of notes per chord is not consistent, indicating a lack of attention to the voice-leading of the inner parts.

Example 4.23   IBc, P. 120, ms attributed to Stradella, *Regole*, pp. 33–6

Gasparini is one of the few composers to harmonize the scales in a more 'modern', tonal way (Example 4.24): 'Per assicurarsi nel modo di circolar tutti i Toni, ne dimostrerò tutti gli esempi, de' quali lo studioso impossessandosi ne troverà gran giovamento' ['In order to gain confidence in moving around all the keys, I will give all the examples; in mastering them, the scholar will obtain great benefit'].

Example 4.24   F. Gasparini, *L'armonico pratico*, p. 83

This harmonization is repeated in twenty other keys in order for the harpsichordist to gain familiarity with these progressions. Gasparini was not the only composer to be experimenting with enharmonicism at this time; it could be speculated that this novelty in the writing of the period pushed Gasparini to publish a way of harmonizing scales in all the keys – an example of basso continuo and its teaching adapting to changes in musical style. He had already experimented with extreme modulations and enharmonic chords in his cantata *Ed ecco in fine* (Example 4.25). Other authors were also writing in a similar manner. Francesco Conti's recitatives, for example, are very extreme in the keys they go through (Example 4.26).[21]

Harmonies in Recitatives

The rules of accompaniment also cover the harmonization of recitatives, when the harmony changes above a held note.

Sangiovanni writes: 'Note legate da Recitativo con le loro false: Quanto più saranno piene, e raddoppiate tanto le Consonanze, quanto le loro false, faranno migliore effetto' ['Tied notes in recitative and their dissonances: the more these consonances and dissonances are full and doubled, the better the effect will be'].[22] He specifies that both the consonances and dissonances should be doubled. His wording is similar to that of Gasparini who, however, advises that only the dissonances should be doubled: 'Queste false più saranno piene, e raddioppiate faranno migliore effetto' ['These dissonances, the fuller and more doubled they are, the better the effect will be'].

When the harmony changes from $\frac{5}{3}$ to $\frac{4}{2}$ over a pedal note, both Gasparini and Sangiovanni add the fifth and the seventh (Example 4.27a). Roma N.1 in addition to the fifth and seventh suggests a ninth would also sound good; the anonymous author reiterates the complete figuring, as Example 4.27b shows.

The *regole d'accompagnamento* call unanimously for full chords and rich harmonies. No manuscript or printed source displays other than minor divergences; the diffusion of the same material is shown by there being many quotes and repeats from one source to another. It it clear that this was the way continuo was taught throughout Italy, and much authority can rightfully be attributed to this manner of performance.

The 'partimenti'

Alessandro Scarlatti's exercises that follow his *Regole* are formulas for realizing standard bass lines. Under the heading *Per accompagnare il cembalo, ò organo, ò*

---

21   Francesco Conti, *David, Azione sacra per musica* (performed in Vienna, 1724).
22   Sangiovanni, *Primi ammaestramenti della musica figurata*, p. 28.

Example 4.25 F. Gasparini, *Cantate da camera a voce sola*, 'Ed ecco in fine'

Example 4.26   F. Conti, *David, Azione sacra per musica*

Example 4.27a F. Gasparini, *L'armonico pratico*, p. 90

Example 4.27b Roma N.1, *Regole per accompagnar sopra la parte*, Chapter XXI, *Regole diverse*, folio 57v

altro stromento[23] there are many exercises for *partimenti* – that is, figured basses with no melody placed above. *Partimenti* were exercises in counterpoint and harmony where often, at the beginning of the piece, an incipit for the realization of the right hand would be marked – this theme was to be continued throughout the exercise, evolving the pupil's ability to adapt these formulas in order to play a well-structured composition with both harmonic and melodic invention from the bass alone. *Partimenti* were part of the general training of the harpsichordist for performance of all types of harpsichord works, both solo and in accompaniment; this technique was then incorporated in playing basso continuo with the *regole d'accompagnamento* (see p. 85).

According to the *regole*, the sevenths in Example 4.28, as the bass moves by leap, are reiterated at each crotchet, not held over. The richness of harmony exemplified in this figuring demands that full chords be played; there are so many dissonances that often it is not possible to prepare and resolve all voices correctly as many authors warned (pp. 82–3), yet the result is most successful.

Example 4.28   A. Scarlatti, GBLbl, Add.14244, folio 42v

Franceso Durante and Gaetano Greco were two other Neapolitan writers of *Partimenti* and most of their exercises include the incipit for the right hand. When these right-hand incipits are given they are often more in the style of a solo harpsichord piece rather than an accompaniment; their study improves the harpsichordist's improvisatory techniques, as in Example 4.29.[24] How this skill was used in accompaniment is discussed on p. 122.

Compositions Taking the Form of Accompaniments

Gasparini wrote 'figurandosi che l'accompagnare è un comporre all'improvviso' ['think of accompaniment as improvised composition'], telling the keyboard

---

[23]   This heading appears in the London manuscript; in other versions the title differs slightly.

[24]   Francesco Durante, *Partimenti, ossia intero studio di numerati per ben suonare il cembalo* (IBc, EE.171).

Example 4.29   F. Durante, *Partimenti*, Museo internazionale e biblioteca della musica di Bologna (EE.171)

player that they must accompany in many different ways, changing the style of their realization according to the characteristics and requirements of each person they are accompanying. Yet fully composed accompaniments – as opposed to instant, improvisatory accompaniments or fully written-out realizations – were certainly written. Alessandro Scarlatti's *Da sventura à sventura* (1690) is an example of fully written keyboard composition and, as such, offers no exemplar of what is an accompaniment following the *regole* and with the aims discussed here (Example 4.30).[25] A composition in the accompaniment form by a master composer and performer for a specific work cannot be taken as a model for the performance of accompaniment in general; rather than offering or following rules for style in accompaniments it is an extraordinary exception, a composition conceived and fixed by the composer for all future performance, that acts as an accompaniment.

---

[25] Alessandro Scarlatti, *Da sventura à sventura* (INc, MS 34.5.2).

Example 4.30 A. Scarlatti, *Da sventura à sventura*

The Favouring of Harmony over Counterpoint

The *regole* show a strong, supportive and harmonically rich style of accompaniment. It is, most of all, a chordal accompaniment, with little room for melodic invention from the harpsichordist (melodic accompaniment is discussed from p. 121). Chords usually are placed only on strong beats, enhancing the rules of accentuation within the bar, although the performer is left with the possibility of changing this accentuation for variety. In practice it is possible to play a powerful accompaniment in this style, influencing the accentuation in the bar by varying the number of notes and dissonances in each chord according to the meaning of words or dramatic context. Yet the various merits of harmonic accompaniments and contrapuntal accompaniments were still under discussion, just as in the previous century (p. 54).

At the beginning of the Introduction to *L'armonico pratico* Gasparini writes 'Per accompagnare ... è necessario il possesso di tutte le buone regole del Contrapunto' ['In order to accompany ... it is necessary to master all the good rules of counterpoint'], although he later specifies that indeed it is possible to learn from his method of teaching without knowing counterpoint: 'Per chi poi vorrà alla prima, senza altro studio d'Intavolatura, o di Contrapunto imparar di accompagnare, hò procurato di stender una maniera facile fin dalla prima cognizione de' tasti, col modo di formar le Consonanze' ['For those who would like to learn accompaniment at their first attempt, without any other study of *intavolatura* or of counterpoint, I have sought to describe an easy method from the first acquaintance with the keys, including the way to form consonances']. He states explicitly that although it is best to have a knowledge of counterpoint, nonetheless he will teach how to play basso continuo harmonically.

The manuscript Roma N.1 goes further; whilst discussing the 'new' way of playing with *acciaccature* it explicitly states that correct counterpoint and correct voice-leading are no longer the most important factors in the accompaniment; indeed, the performer should 'abandon scruples' and, even if this does entail playing consecutive fifths and octaves, always play with full harmonies:

Si nella pienezza dell'armonia, che nella falsità nel qual modo non si può camminare molto con scrupoli circa il sfuggire gl'errori, come le due quinte, o le due ottave. Seguita sia le parti, et i cattivi movimenti; poichè per sonar pieno, bisognerà concedere qualche cosa, che non possa stare nelle regole del ben suonare e nelle false non si potrà tanto osservare, che siano legate prima, e poi risolute.

[Both in the fullness of harmony, and in the dissonances, in which case one cannot go very far with scruples about avoiding errors such as two fifths or two octaves. This [full playing] results both in [bad] parts, and bad movements [of the parts]; for in order to play fully it is necessary to concede something, which falls outside the rules of good playing, and it will not be possible to prepare and resolve dissonances.]

The author acknowledges that the resulting accompaniment will be full of formal mistakes and incorrect voice-leading but considers these to be worthy sacrifices to a richer, harmonic accompaniment. Gasparini allows 'raddoppiamento delle consonanze', doubling of consonances, recommending the harpsichordist should 'adoprar più tasti che si può, per cavar maggior armonia' – use as many keys as possible, to gain the most harmony, without concern for the number of voices or any consecutive fifths and octaves that might result in the inner parts; he is concerned only that these should not occur between the outer parts – in order to prevent this he recommends contrary motion. As Tagliavini explains, Gasparini argues that any 'bad' movement of the inner voices, including consecutives, can be justified by the parts crossing.[26] Gasparini writes:

> Nè si osserva così esattamente che nel mezzo non vi siano le ottave e le quinte, benchè procedino con l'istesso moto, perché si suppone siano salvate col cambiamento delle parti, come nelle composizioni a 5, a 6, e 8 voci, dove le parti composte si raddoppiano le consonanze una con l'altra, ma cangiandosi in modo che tra di loro non vi siamo i disordini proibiti dalle buone regole del contrappunto.[27]

> [Nor does one watch so carefully that in the middle [parts] there are no octaves and fifths, even if these [parts] proceed with the same movement, because it is presumed they are saved by the crossing over of parts; as happens in compositions for 5, 6, and 8 voices, where the composed parts double their consonances one with another, yet change between themselves in such a way as to avoid the errors forbidden by the correct rules of counterpoint.]

The instructions on playing harmonically were also in contrast to the required manner of accompanying on the organ in church music, for a clear distinction is always made between styles of accompaniment on the two keyboard instruments.

Basso Continuo Accompaniment on the Organ

While throughout the centuries accompaniment on the organ remained relatively immune to the many stylistic changes in composition that shape style in realization on other continuo instruments, in practical terms the organ responds well to adjustments in voices and changes in the density of the inner voices made by the continuo player (as composers were already describing in the previous century, see p. 56). Nonetheless, Gasparini insists upon a more 'composed' accompaniment for the organ:

---

[26] Luigi Ferdinando Tagliavini, '*L'armonico pratico al cimbalo* – Lettura critica', *Quaderni della Rivista Italiana di Musicologia 6* (1981), pp. 133–55.

[27] Gasparini, *L'armonico pratico*, p. 87.

Distinguo però l'accompagnare in Organo, dove sarà bene servirsi di questa maniera piena nelle cose a più voci ripiene; ma in Concertini a solo, o due Voci, è molto meglio con le sole pure Consonanze necessarie, senza raddoppiamenti, e come se si sonassero le quattro parti, il che fatto con aggiustatezza, sarà il più pulito, e regolato modo, che si possa fare; figurandosi, che l'accompagnare è un comporre all'improvviso.[28]

[However, I distinguish accompaniment on the organ, where it is best to follow this full manner [of accompanying] in pieces with many voices; but in *concertini* with one or two voices it is much better to use the sole pure necessary consonances, without doubling, as if playing in four parts. If this is done with care, it will be the neatest and most controlled way possible; think of accompaniment as improvised composition.]

He reserves a four-part 'structured' realization for the accompaniment of few voices allowing, however, the usual doublings necessary for the *maniera piena* – the full style of playing – in the accompaniment of many voices, or large ensembles.

The rules of counterpoint can be respected only when playing the organ because of its sustained sound; the sound of the harpsichord, dying more quickly, is only kept alive by playing many notes, frequently repeated, as so often described. As Geminiani wrote: 'the Art of Accompaniment chiefly consists in rendering the Sounds of the Harpsichord lasting'.[29] The resultant differences between playing on the harpsichord and playing on the organ are very marked both in solo repertoire and in basso continuo accompaniment. A most obvious example in the solo repertoire of the period is Alessandro Scarlatti's *Toccata sesta*, entitled *Toccata per organo, e per cembalo / dov'è arpeggio, sù l'organo è tenuta* – that is, to be arpeggiated when played on the harpsichord, held when played on the organ – specifically responding to this distinction between the two instruments (Example 4.31).[30]

Manfredini, as late 1775, is still adamant that the style of accompaniment should be different on harpsichord and organ: 'Egli è certo che l'Organo essendo uno strumento, il quale può ritenere il suono, va trattato diversamente dal Cembalo, non solo accompagnando; ma ancora sonando d'Intavolatura' ['Certainly the organ, being an instrument that can hold sound, should be treated differently from the harpsichord, not only when accompanying, but also when playing from an *intavolatura*'].[31]

---

[28]   Gasparini, *L'armonico pratico*, p. 88.

[29]   Francesco Geminiani, *The Art of Accompaniment or A new and well digested method to learn to perform the Thorough Bass on the Harpsichord* (London, 1754), The Explanation of the Examples.

[30]   See Luigi Ferdinando Tagliavini, 'L'arte di "non lasciar vuoto lo strumento": appunti sulla prassi cembalistica italiana nel Cinque- e Seicento', *Rivista Italiana di Musicologia*, vol. 10 (1975): 360–78, for a discussion of the differences between organ and harpsichord and their implications in performance.

[31]   Vincenzo Manfredini, *Regole armoniche* (Bologna, 1775), p. 63.

Example 4.31   A. Scarlatti, *Toccata sesta*

That composers distinguish between a more formally correct style for the organ and a richer and fuller style for playing the harpsichord not only strengthens both styles of playing but also emphasizes how special are the performance requirements of the harpsichord, instantiated by the need to keep the sound alive.

Performance Achievements of the Regole d'accompagnamento

The characteristic lack of figures in Italian music and the Italian skill at realizing the bass without figures from a score or even from a bass line alone – the product of the study of the *regole* and *Partimenti* (see p. 76), and the inventiveness, responsiveness and grace that this gave – was admired throughout Europe, as Jean Jacques Rousseau comments: 'Les Italiens méprisent les chiffres; la Partition même leur est peu nécessaire: la promptitude e la finesse de leur oreille y supplée, e ils accompagnent fort bien sans tout cet appareil' ['The Italians are contemptuous of figures; a score for them is hardly necessary; their promptness and the finesse of their ears suffice, and they accompany very well without all that equipment'].[32] This Italian contempt for figures is well expressed by Vivaldi in the third movement of the Concerto in A major for violin and strings RV 340.

---

[32]   Jean Jacques Rousseau, *Dictionnaire de musique* (Paris, 1753), Accompagnement.

He illustrates explicitly how it is essential to have a knowledge of the harmony implied by the movement of the bass, in other words of the *regole*, quite aside from basic harmonic knowledge; the 7–6 suspensions he begins marking were so taken for granted, even though not included in the violin part, that he felt justified in figuring in an unnaturally large hand, ending the marking with the words *per li coglioni* (Example 4.32).

Example 4.32   A. Vivaldi, Concerto in A major for violin and strings RV 340, Saxon State and University Library (Mus. 2389-O-43)

The elegance and sobriety of Italian accompaniment is noted too by Rousseau:

> Les Italiens ne veulent pas qu'on entende rien dans l'*Accompagnement*, ni dans la Basse, qui puisse distraire un moment l'oreille du Chant; e leurs *Accompagnements* sont toujours dirigés sur ce principe, que le plaisir e l'attention s'évaporent en se partageant.[33]

> [The Italians do not want one to hear anything in the accompaniment, or in the bass, that might distract the ear from the voice for a moment; their accompaniments are always directed by the principle that pleasure and attention evaporate if they are separated.]

Italian accompaniment was not always laden with the extravagant ornamentation for which it was most famous (discussed from p. 87) – the Italian continuo player was both willing and able to play powerfully yet subtly, and following the *regole d'accompagnamento* was the means by which this was achieved.

---

[33]   Rousseau, *Dictionnaire de musique*, Accompagnement.

Ornamentation

Basso continuo encompasses a great variety of styles of ornamentation: the differences between right-hand and left-hand ornamentation, the well-documented practice of *acciaccature*, and the distinctive impact on harpsichord sonorities these ornaments have are all important contributing factors to continuo playing. Having mastered the *regole d'accompagnamento* the continuo player must then know how to spread chords and introduce dissonances, distinguishing between those that are held and those that must be released quickly – what follows applies principally to the harpsichord.

Arpeggio

The spreading of a chord to form an arpeggio is an intrinsic part of harpsichord technique; the contrasts it can achieve when used skilfully in performance are extreme. The arpeggio is, of course, closely linked to *acciaccature* (p. 89); when a chord is spread, and *acciaccature* are added to the chord, the length and type of arpeggio played are crucial to the effect of the accompaniment – for this reason they are considered together, and both as ornamentation. Manfredini writes:

> Le Acciaccature sono alcuni intervalli, che accompagnando si aggiungono agli Accordi, per ritrar da questi un'Armonia frizzante, e briosa ... Queste Acciaccature rendono ancora un effetto migliore quando gli Accordi sono eseguiti in forma d'Arpeggio, come suol farsi Accompagnando i Recitativi.[34]

> [Acciaccature are those intervals that are added to chords when accompanying to gain a sparkling and lively harmony ... These acciaccature give an even better effect when the chords are performed as an Arpeggio, as is usual when accompanying recitatives.]

Arpeggi are also a vehicle *per non lasciar lo strumento vuoto, per tener sempre viva l'armonia delle note* – meaning to not leave the instrument empty, and for the harmony always to be alive, the most common phrases used in contemporary treatises.

Gasparini expresses his contempt for the *Suonatorelli* and the *Suonatoroni* – derogatory references to a performing musician – when urging the need to use the arpeggio elegantly both in solo repertoire and in continuo playing; it is to be used only in well-defined places and circumstances, not simply applied liberally at any point in the music:

> Per introdur gli accompagnamenti nè Recitativi con qualche sorte di buon gusto si deve distender le Consonanze quasi arpeggiando, ma non di continuo; perchè quando si è fatta sentire l'armonia della nota, si deve tener fermi i tasti, e lasciar, che il cantore si sodisfi, e canti col suo comodo, e secondo che porta l'espressiva delle parole, e non

---

[34] Manfredini, *Regole armoniche*, p. 62.

infastidirlo, o disturbarlo con un continuo arpeggio, o tirare di passaggi in sù, e in giù, come fanno alcuni, non sò s'io dica, Suonatoroni, o Suonatorelli, che per far pompa della loro velocità di mano; credendola bizzaria, fanno una confusione.[35]

[In order to introduce accompaniments in the recitatives with some form of good taste one should unfold the consonances almost arpeggiando, but not continuously; because when the harmony of the note has been heard one should hold the keys still, and allow the singer to sing to their own satisfaction and convenience, according to what is involved by the word's expressiveness, without irritating or disturbing the singer with a continuous arpeggio, or passages up and down as it is done by some – what shall I call them – *Suonatoroni*, or *Suonatorelli*, who in order to show off their speed of hand, fall into a confusion which they mistake for exoticism.]

This strong warning against using the arpeggio to excess, particularly to the point of obscuring the vocal line is found also in Sangiovanni and in most other sources.

An example of how the arpeggio was used for loud and obtrusive effects correctly can be found in Act II Scene 3 of Vivaldi's opera *Giustino* (Example 4.33), where an approaching sea-monster is represented by harpsichords in 'arpeggio continuo'.[36]

Example 4.33   A. Vivaldi, *Giustino*, Act II Scene 3

Vivaldi considered the effect of continuous arpeggiation so special he specified when he wanted that effect. The indication 'il cembalo arpeggio' appears in

---

[35]   Gasparini, *L'armonico pratico*, p. 91.
[36]   Antonio Vivaldi, *Giustino* RV 717 (performed Rome, 1724).

the Adagio molto from *L'autunno*;[37] to play arpeggi against strings playing delicately with mutes is, of course, a completely different use of the instrument from representing a sea monster. Indications for arpeggi appear in very diverse circumstances and can refer to very different kinds of effects, being used as a device to increase volume, or as a means of keeping the harmony alive; it is left to the continuo player to judge how to arpeggiate in the most appropriate manner.

Acciaccature

In 1771, Burney wrote from Venice: 'No one will, I believe, at present, deny the necessity of *dischord* in the composition of music in parts.'[38] It is interesting to consider how dissonances, and discord, came to be such an essential part of Italian music.

Benedetto Marcello, writing over 60 years earlier, circa 1705, expresses concern that the new trend of playing with *acciaccature* should not grow to the point where the *acciaccature* themselves are considered as harmony notes, and severely advises the reader to study the harpsichord works of Pasquini and Frescobaldi as examples of the best harpsichord music writing:

> L'acciaccatura è accidente di suono, non sostanza di contrapunto, come sono le appoggiature, li modi di buon cantare, eccetera che da Moderni si scrivono, e tale acciaccatura suole pratticarsi particolarmente ne Recitativi, Cadenze, progressioni di Tuono à Tuono, eccetera come più diffusamente nell'Armonico Prattico al Cimbalo di Francesco Gasparini mio Maestro al Cap. nono.[39]

> [The *acciaccatura* is a sound occurrence, not [of the] substance of counterpoint, as are *appoggiature*, the practices of good singing etcetera which are written out by Moderns; and such *acciaccatura* is practised especially in recitatives, cadences, progressions etcetera, as is discussed in greater detail in the ninth chapter of the *Armonico pratico al cimbalo* by my teacher Francesco Gasparini.]

Marcello's teacher Gasparini was a pupil of Pasquini, widely regarded as the greatest accompanist of all time; Marcello points out that Pasquini too was clear that, although beautiful, *acciaccature* should not be considered as part of counterpoint. In Chapter IX of *L'armonico pratico*, Gasparini discusses *acciaccature* and their effect within the arpeggio:

> Nel distender, come dissi la Consonanza piena, si potrà all'Ottava nella mano destra toccar quasi fuggendo il semitono suo vicino sotto la detta ottava ... toccandolo con

---

[37] Antonio Vivaldi, Concerto in F major *L'autunno*, RV 293, *Il cimento dell'armonia e dell'inventione Op. VIII n.3* (Amsterdam [1725]).

[38] Charles Burney, *The Present State of Music in France and Italy* (London, 1771), p. 152.

[39] Benedetto Marcello, *Lettera familiare* (Venice, ? after 1704), p. 45.

certa destrezza nel medemo tempo in forma di mordente, anzi un poco prima, ma lasciarlo immediate, perchè non offenda l'udito, ma dia una certa grazia. Che perciò vien detto mordente, a guisa del morso di un piccolo Animaletto, che appena morde subito lascia, e non offende.

[In unfolding the full consonance, as I said, [in addition] to the octave in the right hand one can touch fleetingly the nearest semitone below this octave ... touching it quickly at the same time – indeed a little sooner – in the manner of a *mordente* with a certain swiftness, but leaving it immediately so that it does not offend the ear, but adds grace. This is why it is called *mordente*, like the bite of a little animal, one that bites but immediately releases, and does not harm.]

Gasparini describes where it is appropriate to place *acciaccature*, with examples. Tagliavini, in his article '*L'armonico pratico al cimbalo* – Lettura critica',[40] gives an exhaustive, codified explanation of Gasparini's rules on *acciaccature*, with examples and references to sonatas by Domenico Scarlatti that illustrate the use of these techniques. Eight examples of where and how it is appropriate to include *acciaccature* in continuo realization are given by Gasparini.

Example 1 Here, an example of the resolution of a $^6_4$ chord is given:

right hand	6	5
	4	3
left hand	6	5
	4	

The $^6_4$ chord is doubled in both hands, but the fourth is only resolved in the right, leaving the fourth of the left hand unresolved – Gasparini says of this technique: 'si riceve un'armonia assai grata, ed è una specie (come molti suonatori dicono) di acciaccatura' ['the result is a very beautiful harmony, and this is a type of *acciaccatura* (as many players call it)'].

Example 2 *Acciaccature* sound good on dominant sevenths at cadence points, in the right hand as well as in both hands: 'serve alle cadenze e ogni volta che le note con la settima vogliono la terza maggiore, restando tra la detta terza maggiore e la quinta unita la quarta per acciaccatura' ['[dominant sevenths] are useful at cadence points; and every time these sevenths take a major third, this third and fifth should be joined by the fourth, in the manner of an *acciaccatura*']. The interval between the third and the fifth should be filled with an *acciaccatura* while the chord is being spread. Domenico Scarlatti uses this technique in his Sonata K. 215, bar 42.

---

[40]   Here the Scarlatti Sonata examples are taken from Tagliavini's work.

Example 3 Acciaccature can be placed on leading notes. The chord should consist of the diminished fifth together with the minor sixth; between the octave and the tenth an *acciaccatura* should be formed with the ninth (as well as with the fourth). An example of this can be found in D. Scarlatti's Sonata K. 64, bar 9.

Example 4 To a chord on the second degree, that is with a minor third and a major sixth, a fourth and a seventh should be added. D. Scarlatti uses this technique in his Sonata K. 175, bars 22 and 24.

Example 5 Having explained the principles, Gasparini encourages 'the harmony scholar':

> Doverà poi lo Studioso Armonico insegnarsi di ritrovar tasteggiando queste, e simili acciaccature per altri Toni di ogni genere ... ed anche trovarne di altra sorte, come appunto io studiando ritrovai potersi fare in una falsa un'acciaccatura raddoppiata con toccar quattordici tasti in un colpo.

> [The harmony scholar will then have to teach himself how to find again, feeling the keyboard, these and similar *acciaccature* for other keys of every kind ... and also to find new ones, precisely as I have discovered in my studies that in a dissonance you can play a double *acciaccatura* touching fourteen keys at a stroke.]

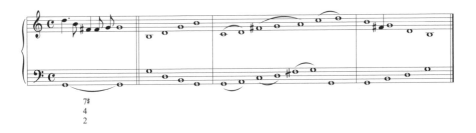

Example 4.34 **F. Gasparini, *L'armonico pratico, Delle false de i recitativi, e del modo di far acciaccature*, p. 97**

Example 4.34 shows the most extravagant of the chords he describes – fourteen notes to be played simultaneously. He goes on to explain how this chord should be realized:

> Per formar questa Acciaccatura bisogna con estremi d'ambe le mani toccar due tasti con un sol dito, cioè con l'Auricolare, e con il Pollice. Questo però serva più di bizzarria, che di esempio, o regola generale, potendosi qualche volta usare, ma distinguer tempo, luogo, e persone.

[To form this *acciaccatura* you must touch two keys with with one finger using the extremities of both hands, that is with the little finger and the thumb. This however is given more as an exceptional case than as an example or a general rule, since it can be used occasionally but when time, place and performers are considered appropriate.]

Example 6 When there is a $^6_{4\sharp}$ chord on the fourth degree, the fifth should be played between the fourth and the sixth as an *acciaccatura*:

Alle note che hanno seconda e quarta maggiore che, come si è detto, non va una senza l'altra, e vogliono ancor la sesta maggiore, si unirà tra la 4a e la 6a per acciaccatura la quinta nel mezzo, e sarà bene.

[Notes that take a major second and fourth (as we have said there cannot be one without the other) and also take a major sixth, should be joined by an *acciaccatura* between the 4th and 6th, which will sound good.]

Example 7 Gasparini describes an *acciaccatura* formed of two, three or four keys played one next to the other ('due, tre o quattro tasti uniti uno appresso l'altro') which can be used often, and especially on notes that take a major sixth.

Example 8 Gasparini calls this a 'passo particolare', a special movement: here the bass is on the sixth degree and then falls to the dominant, while the voice forms an augmented second with the bass. In such an instance the bass should be accompanied by a third (against which the voice forms an *acciaccatura*), an augmented fourth, and a sixth; he advises the player to double this in the left hand as well. An example of this is found in D. Scarlatti's Sonata K. 175, bars 66–68.

The rules given in Roma N.1 give valuable information on playing with *acciaccature*; an aria with a fully written out realization (the difficulties this entails are noted on pp. 2–3), including *acciaccature*, is given, and the paragraph that precedes the aria gives good practical indications on how to play in this manner. It is worth quoting in full:

Si è messo grandemente in uso hoggidì il suonar pieno, quanto si può, e con false che dilettino, cercando in questo solamente il gusto dell'orecchio. Si nella pienezza dell'armonia, che nella falsità nel qual modo non si può camminare molto con scrupoli circa il sfuggire gl'errori, come le due quinte, o le due ottave. Seguita sia le parti, et i cattivi movimenti; poichè per sonar pieno, bisognerà concedere qualche cosa, che non possa stare nelle regole del ben suonare e nelle false non si potrà tanto osservare, che siano legate prima, e poi risolute, e nell'ordine delle consonanze non si potrà camminare così regolato, e basterà riguardarsi di non fare la 2.da, 5.ta, e le due ottave seguite frà il basso, et il soprano, perchè essendo si dilettevole questo bel modo di suonare detto comunemente d'acciaccature, l'orecchio resta tanto soddisfatto dalla pienezza dell'armonia, e dalle false, che per godere tal soddisfazzione bisognerà come si è detto lasciar gli scrupoli da parte altrimenti si resterà nell'antico modo di suonar secco, dove con la molta armonia benchè si faccino le due 5.e e le due 8.e frà le parti non restano distinte che possino offendere l'orecchio; se per dar un poco di lume a chi vorrà praticare questo modo, ho messo in intavolatura questa mia arietta, acciò il scolare cognosca da questa come si possa col suo giudizio governare.

Fra le consonanze pongo talvolta alcune dissonanze toccandola e subito lasciandola, e la chiamo mordente quasi un picciol morso d'animaletto, quale appena ponga il dente e poi subito lo toglie, e se ad'alcuno piacesse più tenere, che levare la dissonanza, starà in suo arbitro.

[It has become extremely fashionable nowadays to play as fully as possible, and with pleasing dissonances, seeking only the ear's delight – both in the fullness of harmony, and in the dissonances, in which case one cannot go very far with scruples about avoiding errors such as two fifths or two octaves. This [full playing] results both in [bad] parts, and bad movements [of the parts]; for in order to play fully it is necessary to concede something, which falls outside the rules of good playing, and it will not be possible to prepare and resolve dissonances, and in the ordering of consonances one will not be able to proceed according to the rules; it is sufficient to be careful to avoid consecutive seconds, fifths and octaves between the bass and the soprano, because this way of playing, commonly called *acciaccature*, is so delightful, and the ear remains so satisfied by the fullness of harmony, that to enjoy such gratification it is necessary, as we have said, to leave aside all scruples, otherwise we are left with the old way of playing *secco*; with all the harmony, although the two fifths and the two octaves are played between the parts, there remain no distinct parts that can offend the ear. In order to enlighten a little those who might practise this manner, I have put this little aria of mine in *intavolatura*, so that the scholar might know from it how to govern [this style] with his judgement. Among consonances sometimes I place some dissonances, touching them and releasing them at once; I call this *mordente*, like a little bite by a small animal who might just use its teeth and then immediately withdraw; though if someone wished to hold the dissonance rather than leave it, he could do so at his own discretion.]

After almost a hundred years (p. 54) a change from the old style 'antico modo di suonar secco' where voice-leading was well observed and no 'extra' notes were added, is still having to be argued; as is that correct voice-leading must be abandoned and the ear satisfied with the fullness of harmonies thus created. The harpsichordist must 'leave scruples behind' and play fully; it is sufficient to guard against two consecutive seconds, fifths or octaves between the bass and the soprano. Roma N.1 is less precise than Gasparini (quoted on p. 83), but they both say the same thing: when a full realization is played, 'bad' movements between the inner parts are inaudible (Example 4.35).

Despite the outlandish appearance of Example 4.35, its author should be praised for having tried to write down what is impossible to annotate; a close reading of this accompaniment, in conjunction with the ample introduction and a consideration of Gasparini's teachings discussed above, shows that every note and unusual feature of this accompaniment can be justified. The right hand is in the same range as the singer, indeed often doubles the vocal line, undoubtedly its correct range. Dissonances are doubled in both hands, as is widely recommended. The author distinguishes between notes added to the chord that are not marked

Example 4.35   Roma N.1, *Regole per accompagnar sopra la parte*, 'Sono un certo spiritello', *Aria*, folio 66

in the figures and *acciaccature*, which he always annotates as lasting for half the value of the length of the bass note. The leading note always takes a $^6_5$ chord (bar 1, 3rd crotchet; bar 2, 4th crotchet), as described by Gasparini in his third example (p. 91); the E in bar 2 and the B♭ in bar 3 are all marked 6 but are realized as $^6_4$, and in bar 4 the E is realized as $^6_5$. The *acciaccature*, all marked short, are examples of what Gasparini describes when he talks of two, three or four notes one next to the other – these are quick and the dissonances do not need to be resolved.

The author of this aria discusses whether *acciaccature* should be held or not: 'se ad'alcuno piacesse più tenere, che levare la dissonanza, starà in suo arbitro' ['though if someone wished to hold the dissonance rather than leave it, he could do so at his own discretion']. He recommends letting go of the note immediately; nevertheless, he adds that if the performer wishes to hold the *acciaccature* for longer, it is legitimate to do so. Held *acciaccature* are found throughout the Italian harpsichord repertoire of the 1700s. Alessandro Scarlatti's *Toccata per cembalo d'ottava stesa*, illustrates them well (Example 4.36).[41]

Example 4.36   A. Scarlatti, *Toccata per cembalo d'ottava stesa*, Adagio, bars 245–249

---

[41]   Alessandro Scarlatti, *Toccata per cembalo d'ottava stesa*, in *Primo e secondo libro di Toccate del Sig. Cavagliere Alessandro Scarlatti* (Naples, [1724]).

Here are more examples of *acciaccature* that act like unresolved dissonances; but the effect these chords produce is different from the shorter *acciaccature* of the previous examples. Whereas before they make a strong, fast dissonance, here, because they are longer, they create a web of dissonant sounds above which the right hand plays. Scarlatti's *Toccata* shows that the *acciaccatura* is not necessarily short, indeed the longer it is the stronger its effect; it can also be held as dissonant harmony.

Gasparini describes how to obtain this effect: 'Bisogna con la destra adoprar tutte le dita, e alle volte si toccano due tasti con un sol dito, per lo più col pollice' ['One must use all the fingers of the right hand, and sometimes touch two keys with a single finger, often the thumb'].[42] In the penultimate chord of Example 4.36, it is necessary for the thumb to play both the D and the E; of course, if the thumb is playing two notes it is impossible to separate them, so they both must be long.

Burney, musing on these issues of dissonances, wrote:

> If, for instance, the five sounds c. d. e. f. g., are all struck at the same instant on the harpsichord, provided the d and the f are taken off soon, and the three others remain, the ear will not suffer much by the first shock. Or, still further; if, instead of the five sounds above-mentioned, the following are struck; c. d.♯. e. f♯. g. and the d. and f♯ are not held on so long as the rest, all will end to the satisfaction of the offended ear.[43]

Continuo players were expected to add to the composition with 'extra' harmony notes, either held or short, for as Gasparini said about dissonances: 'pare che diano campo al buon cantore di meglio esprimere gli affetti e il buon gusto delle composizioni' ['It seems that they allow a good singer to express the *affetti* and the *buon gusto* of compositions better'].

Trills

One of the earliest examples of written-out trills in continuo playing is given by Lorenzo Penna.[44] Book 3 of *Li primi albori musicali* is dedicated entirely to basso continuo (the previous two having been on general theory and counterpoint respectively), and the examples of how to trill are combined with the examples on how to harmonize unfigured basses, showing that Penna is referring specifically to trills in basso continuo, rather than teaching about trills in general harpsichord playing.

Of those rules referring specifically to trills, Rule 11 of the first chapter says:

---

[42] Gasparini, *L'armonico pratico*, p. 94.

[43] Burney, *The Present State of Music in France and Italy*, p. 153.

[44] Lorenzo Penna, *Li primi albori musicali* (Bologna, 1684), book 3.

Che volendo far trilli, questi si formino sù due tasti, cioè sù quello della Nota, ò numero scritto, e il tasto vicino di sopra, fermandosi nel fine sù la Nota, ò numero scritto, avvertendo, che facendoli con la mano sinistra, per ordinario si fanno con il medio, e Indice; mà con la destra, per lo più devono farsi con l'Anulare, e Medio.

[When wishing to trill, these should be formed on two keys, that is the note or number [figure] that is written, and the key above it; [the trill must] stop on the note, or number, that is written; being careful that, when they are done with the left hand, they should normally be played with the middle and index finger; with the right hand, they are to be played with the fourth and middle finger.]

The basic example is given (Example 4.37): the trills start on the note above the main note or figure and end on the main note. In the left hand the trills should be played with the index and middle finger (Example 4.37a); in the right hand trills should be played with the fourth and middle finger: (Example 4.37b).

Example 4.37   L. Penna, *Li primi albori*, p. 152

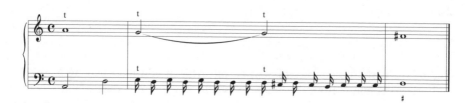

Example 4.37a L. Penna, *Li primi albori*, p. 152

Example 4. 37b L. Penna, *Li primi albori*, p. 152

In Example 4.37b, the trills must run continuously one into another; starting with fingers 4 and 3 the trill can continue untinterruptedly into the second bar using fingers 3 and 2, changing back to 4 3 half way through the second bar in order to end the trill with 3 2. Facility in trilling in all fingers of both hands is required; it is noticeable that in both examples the trill descends a third below the main note before terminating. Another important aspect of these trills is the final repercussions on the same note, a practice derived from vocal ornamentation.

Rule 2 of the fourth chapter says:

Quando la nota, che cala di quarta in giù, ò ascende di quinta in sù, sarà di una battuta, overo di mezza battuta in tempo minore, si potrà fare li seguenti accompagnamenti, essendovi molto tempo cioè: Prima si facci la terza minore con quinta, mà mai terza maggiore, (se non fosse segnata), dopo quarta maggiore e sesta maggiore, formando un trillo su l'ottava, e nona, e un altro trillo sù la quarta, e quinta, e nell'ultima nota formi un altro Trillo sù la quarta, e terza maggiore, calando dopo seconda, e terminando in terza maggiore, ò minore, e quinta.

[When the note that descends by a fourth or ascends by a fifth is a bar long, or half a bar long in smaller time signatures, it should be accompanied in the following way, because there is plenty of time: first play a minor third with a fifth, never a major third (unless indicated), then fourth and major sixth; form a trill on the octave and ninth, and another trill on the fourth and fifth, and on the last note form a trill on the fourth and major third, moving [to the note] below after the second [note], terminating on the major (or minor) third and fifth.]

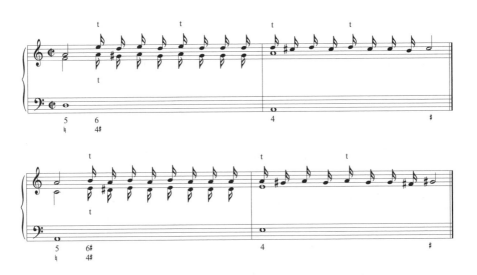

Example 4.38   L. Penna, *Li primi albori*, p. 161

In Example 4.38 the sharpened sixth is missing; these are examples of trills in the right hand, and the left would have filled in harmonically; any left-hand chordal realization would not have been printed because of the difficulty of printing chords with movable type. As in example 4.37 all the trills start on the upper note.

Rule 2 of the fifth chapter says:

> Mentre la Nota, che fa il salto sia d'una battuta, e si habbi tempo, si devon fare gli accompagnamenti seguenti; prima si deve dare terza maggiore, e quinta, poi quarta e sesta maggiore, ò minore conforme alla natura della Cantilena, qual sesta potrà far Trillo con la settima; dopo 4.a e 5.a, con trillo di 5.a e 6.a, e in fine 3.a maggiore con 5.a formando Trillo sù la 4.a e 3.a maggiore della sinistra mano, e con la destra fare 7.a minore e 9.a minore e su l'ultima nota Trillo con la destra sù la 4.a e 3.a maggiore.

> [If the [bass] note that leaps lasts a whole bar, and if there is time, the following accompaniments must be played: first give the major third, and the fifth; then the fourth and sixth, major or minor according to the nature of the melody, and that sixth can make a trill with the seventh; then [play a] fourth and fifth, with a trill of fifth and sixth, and in the end a major third with the fifth forming a trill on the fourth and major third of the left hand, and with the right play a minor seventh and a minor ninth, and on the last note a trill with the right hand on the fourth and major third.]

In Example 4.39, again, Penna does not realize all the notes that are figured; the figured version is nevertheless an example of an unusual $\frac{3}{5}$ cadence, a sound that is rarely heard in performance today. In this example, where the figuring of the penultimate note is very detailed, yet only the left-hand trill is marked, the chord is intended to be fuller than is shown in the example, making the trill less important and more ornamental. In the original, a 9♭ figure is printed above the soprano line, as well as in the figures of the bass, on the last crotchet of the first bar, suggesting that Penna intended the note (E♭) to be the highest in the chord (above the trill), and possibly even doubled in the left hand.

Example 4.39a L. Penna, *Li primi albori: prattica sù le pure note*, p. 164

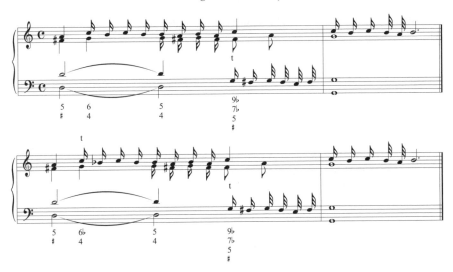

Example 4.39b L. Penna, *Li primi albori: prattica con li trilli*, p. 164

In the eighth chapter, which considers the realization of a fast-moving bass line, Penna gives an important example of where to trill in the bass line: 'Quando il Basso fà una Minima, e dopo due Semiminime seguite per grado, in discendere, si fà la Consonanza con la seconda Semiminima battendo la prima con Trillo, se vorrà' ['When the bass has a minim, and followed by two crotchets that move by step, descending, play a consonance with the second crotchet, striking the first with a trill if desired']. That is, when the bass line descends by step with a minim followed by two crotchets, the chord must be placed on the second crotchet, as the first crotchet is already emphasized because of the trill; in Example 4.40 it can be seen how printing limitations rendered the representation of delicate matters of style difficult; the figure is placed correctly but the right-hand chord is nonetheless on the first crotchet when it should be on the second.

Example 4.40   L. Penna, *Li primi albori*, p. 167

Penna's next mention of trills is in Rule 2 of the ninth chapter, whilst dealing with cadences:

> Quando la Cadenza è fatta con quattro Semiminime, delle quali le trè ultime ascendendo per grado, in tal caso alla prima di quelle si dà la sesta, e ottava con Trillo; alla seconda si dà quinta, e sesta insieme con Trillo; e alla terza si dà con quinta, e Trillo, la terza Maggiore.

> [When the cadence is formed of four crotchets, of which the last three ascend by step, the first crotchet [i.e. the second beat of the bar] takes a sixth, and the octave with a trill; the second crotchet [i.e. the third beat of the bar] takes a fifth and sixth together, with a trill; the third [i.e. the fourth beat of the bar] takes the fifth, and the major third with a trill.]

In Example 4.41, the figure 5 on the second crotchet is printed but should be a 6 following his explanation and the harmony.

> Altre volte si fà con quattro Semiminime, quali paiano formare due Cadenze, in tal caso ancora si dà alla seconda nota terza Maggiore, ò minore secondo la natura della Composizione con Trillo, alla terza nota, quinta, e sesta insieme con Trillo, e alla quarta la terza Maggiore con quinta, e Trillo.

> [Other times four crotchets appear to form two cadences; in these cases the major third or minor third, depending on the nature of the composition, is still given to the second note, with a trill; to the third note, a fifth and sixth together with a trill [should be given], and to the fourth note the major third with the fifth, and trill [should be given].]

In Examples 4.41, 4.42 and 4.43, the realization of the trills is not given, as their performance is by now taken for granted.

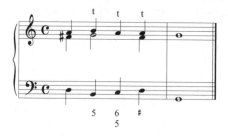

Example 4.41   L. Penna, *Li primi albori*, p. 175

Rule 4 of the ninth chapter says: 'Alcuna volta si fanno quattro Semiminime, che vanno per salti, la terza delle quali fà salto di quarta in sù; alla quale terza si dovrà dare la settima con Trillo, e alla quarta si darà terza Maggiore con quinta, e

Example 4.42   L. Penna, *Li primi albori*, p. 176

Trillo' ['At times four crotchets are played, which move by leap, the third of which leaps upwards by a fourth; the third [crotchet] takes a seventh with a trill; and the fourth takes a major third with a fifth, and trill']. Note the recommendation to add a seventh (Example 4.43).

Example 4.43   L. Penna, *Li primi albori*, p. 176

The only rule in Chapter XII says: 'Si accompagna questa cadenza con dare alla penultima nota la settima e poi sesta Maggiore con Trillo, facendo poi quinta e sesta' ['This cadence should be accompanied by playing a seventh on the penultimate note, then a major sixth with trill, then playing a fifth and a sixth'] (Example 4.44). As in Examples 4.38 and 4.39b, the trills are in fifths, which is particularly strange to the modern ear.

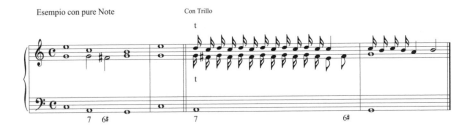

Example 4.44   L. Penna, *Li primi albori*, p. 179

The only rule in Chapter XIII says:

Che sul principio della legatura si dia terza minore, ò maggiore secondo comporta la natura della Cantilena, poi seconda, e quarta insieme, quale quarta deve formar Trillo con quinta, dopo risolvi con la terza accompagnata con quinta falsa, mà con la sinistra mano la Nota fondamentale facci Trillo con seconda, e nell'ultima botta Trilli la destra con quarta, e terza, calando poi seconda, e finendo in consonanza con l'ultima Nota; mà con le Note minute, solo si risolve la seconda con terza. Quì anco si accompagni pure (se vuole) le Dissonanze con le Consonanze della Nota scritta, e aggiunga alla quinta falsa la settima minore, ò Maggiore conforme alla natura della Compositione.

[At the beginning of the tie a minor, or major third should be given, according to the nature of the composition, then the second and fourth together; the fourth must form a trill with the fifth, which then resolves with the third accompanied by a fifth; with the left hand the fundamental note should form a trill with the second, and on the last note the right hand should trill with the fourth, and third, then second, ending with the consonance of the last note; although with the shorter notes only resolve the second with the third. Here if you wish you may also accompany the dissonances with the consonances of the written note, and add the fifth to the minor seventh – or major depending on the nature of the composition.]

Here Penna suggests the addition of further dissonances although these are not illustrated in the example (Example 4.45). This confirms that the chords are intended to be even fuller than in the examples, whose notation is limited by printing problems.

Example 4.45   L. Penna, *Li primi albori,* **p. 181**

Finally Penna advises: 'Suoni assai, studiando di esercitarsi nella velocità, e trilli, si con la mano destra, come la sinistra, perchè così si rompe la mano, e si fà pratico della Tastatura' ['Play a great deal, seeking to practise speed, and trills, both with the right and the left hand, in order to gain agility with the hand and to become acquainted with the keyboard'].

Pannuzzo Pannuzzi's rules, in his *Regole del sonare il basso continuo* reproduce, almost word for word, what Penna writes about trills.[45] On folio 2 v. of his treatise, he gives exactly the same example as does Penna in his fourth chapter, second rule; copies of Penna's trills are found also in the treatise attributed to Stradella and in other anonymous Bologna treatises, confirming that Penna's teachings were emulated.

Bismantova mentions trills when talking about fingerings and implies that it was as frequent to trill with the left hand as it was with the right: 'Volendo far Trilli, con la Mano Sinistra; si faranno con il Medio, et Indice; per ordinario; con la Mano Destra; per lo più devono farsi con l'Anulare, e Medio' ['Trills with the left hand should normally be played with the middle finger and the index finger; with the right hand, mostly trills should be played with the fourth and the middle finger'].[46] Such fingering in the right hand again suggests a long compound trill as Penna exemplifies (p. 96), as it would be more practical to use fingers 2 and 3, or even 2 and 4.

Sonorities foreign to modern ears are produced by the trills Penna describes. His trills are not particularly hard to play, raising queries as to whether he was producing merely an exhaustive list of possibilities rather than a guide to performance; more interestingly, there may be an attempt to carry over the unusual trilling practices from the solo harpsichord repertoire.

Similarity to trills in solo music The regularity with which trills similar to Penna's appear in solo repertoire increases their performance credibility; modern lack of familiarity with the body of keyboard works particularly of lesser-known Italian composers may contribute to their absence from modern continuo realizations. Also, the word *trillo* holds a variety of meanings, and should not be associated with only one type of ornament, as these examples (Examples 4.46–4.50) of different types of 'trill' taken from very different genres of harpsichord music demonstrate.

The *Battaglia* and *Colascione* (Example 4.49 and 4.50), although unusual pieces in themselves, make extensive use of the repeated notes in the trill; indeed in the *Colascione* the trill is one of the most important features of the piece. The trills of Storace and Strozzi are very similar to Penna's and work well in context, demonstrating that the trills Penna describes are in keeping with the Italian style. There are fewer solo harpsichord treatises than there are continuo treatises; it is telling that the content of both kinds is comparable and often interchangeable, indicating that even when accompanying the harpsichord retains many characteristics of its solo uses.

Trills in the bass line In the anonymous Bologna manuscript *Regole per imparare à sonare il cimbalo, ò organo* (dated 1714), the author prescribes an unusually

---

45 Pannuzzo Pannuzzi, *Regole del sonare il basso continuo* (IBc, P. 140, c.1700).

46 Bismantova, *Compendio musicale*, p. 87.

Example 4.46   G. Strozzi, *Romanesca*

extravagant number of trills in the bass line.[47] The types of trill the author describes are different from the trills Penna discusses: 'Facendo per tanto lo scolaro perfettamente quanto si è detto, gli si incomincierà ad insegnare di fare il trillo con la mano sinistra, cioè quella che fa il Basso, ò fondamento, e dove deve farlo' ['Once the scholar can play perfectly everything discussed so far, he should begin to be taught how to trill with the left hand, which plays the bass or foundation, and where the trill should be placed']. The author of this treatise describes specifically where it is appropriate to trill in the bass line. The trill can consist of a tone or a semitone; trills can be placed when the bass moves by step, but should not be played when the bass moves by leap. When the bass descends in quavers or semiquavers, a trill on the third note of a set of four is recommended (Example 4.51). If the bass moves in crotchets the trills should start on the first note and continue, placing a trill on every other note (Example 4.52).

The anonymous author writes that, if the bass line rises by step, the trill must involve the semitone above the given note and fall on the last quaver of a set of four. This is illustrated in Example 4.53, where a trill is placed on beat 4 of bars 1, 3 and 5; when the bass descends, the trill is placed on the third note of four, as in Example 4.51. The anonymous author also states that when the hands are playing in thirds, it is right to trill in both hands (Examples 4.54 and 4.55). The author contends that all dotted notes benefit from a trill, adding that cadence points should always be trilled.

Then follow ascending and descending examples in sixths (Example 4.56). The next example (Example 4.57) is figured with sequences of 7–6 and 9–8 suspensions; the instructions are to trill on the resolution, not on the dissonance. This suggests a short trill that lasts only for the duration of a crotchet.

To end, the author recommends the pupil be taught 'qualche Galanteria … e qualche contrapuntino, acciò possa suonare armoniosamente' ['some *galanterie* … and some counterpoint, so that he may play harmoniously']. The style of

---

[47]   *Regole per imparare à sonare il cimbalo, ò organo, 1714* (IBc, P. 132).

Example 4.47 G. Strozzi, *Ancidetemi dell' Arcadelt*

continuo playing this author is describing is very ornate; the trills used here are all short, and their primary function is to embellish a moving bass line. These trills too are unusual to the modern ear – certainly they are more performable than those of Penna or Pannuzzi.

Example 4.48　B. Storace, *Ciaccona*

Example 4.49　Anon., MSS Chigi, Q.IV.28, *Battaglia*

Tonelli's realizations of Corelli's opus V demonstrate further uses of trills in continuo playing.[48] The Adagio of the *Sonata seconda* opens with a trill in the right hand (Example 4.58), and the *Sonata terza*'s opening Adagio has a trill in the right hand of bar 5 (Example 4.59). In both these examples the trill occurs where taste might suggest a less ornamented accompaniment, forcing the solo line into a response. This treatment of the soloist by the continuo player is possibly one of the reasons why later composers (see the discussion on Veracini, p. 128) were determined to limit inappropriate initiatives by the continuo player.

---

[48]　Tonelli, *Della quint'opra d'Arcangiol Corelli / Basso per tasto d'Antonio Tonelli* (IMOe, Mus. F1174); see note 10.

Example 4.50   Anon., MSS Chigi, Q.IV.28, *Colascione*

Example 4.51   IBc, P. 132, *Regole per imparare à sonare il cimbalo, ò organo,*
folio 12v

Example 4.52   IBc, P. 132, *Regole per imparare à sonare il cimbalo, ò organo,*
folio 12v

Example 4.53   IBc, P. 132, *Regole per imparare à sonare il cimbalo, ò organo,* folio 12v

naturali   maggior i   minori   naturale

Example 4.54   IBc, P. 132, *Regole per imparare à sonare il cimbalo, ò organo,* folio 13, *Essempio di ogni sorte di terza per descendere*

naturali   maggior i   minori   naturali

Example 4.55   IBc, P. 132, *Regole per imparare à sonare il cimbalo, ò organo,* folio 13, *Essempio di ogni sorte di terza per ascendere*

Example 4.56   IBc, P. 132, *Regole per imparare à sonare il cimbalo, ò organo,* folio 13v

Example 4.57   IBc, P. 132, *Regole per imparare à sonare il cimbalo, ò organo,* folio 13v

Example 4.58   A. Corelli/A. Tonelli, Opus V, *Sonata seconda*, Adagio

Example 4.59   A. Corelli/A. Tonelli, Opus V, *Sonata terza*, Adagio, bar 5

Divisions and Realizations

Continuo players had always made variations and divisions on the bass line (see pp. 39–42); at the beginning of the 1700s the types of variations that were stylistically acceptable began to be recorded. The style that resulted from this type of interpretation was particularly pleasing to Italians, 'essendo sì dilettevole questo bel modo di suonare' ['as this beautiful way of playing is so pleasing'],[49] but was criticized by French contemporaries; in 1715, Pierre Bonnet wrote:

> In general one hears in [Italian] music only a basso continuo always ornamented, which is often a kind of *batterie*, with chords and arpeggios, which casts dust in the eyes of those who are not connoisseurs, and which, reduced to its simplest form, is equivalent to ours. The basso continuo are only good to show off the hand of those who accompany ...[50]

The Italians were well aware of the problem; Benedetto Marcello comments on the vulgarity with which divisions on the bass line could be executed: 'Il Virtuoso di Violoncello ... nell'Arie spezzerà il Basso a capriccio, variandolo ogni sera, benchè la Variazione non abbia punto che fare con la parte del Musico, o co' Violini' ['The virtuoso of the violoncello ... will break the bass at his pleasure, changing it every evening, although the variation will have nothing to do with his part, or with the violins'].[51] While such statements seem over-forceful, even when referring to the worst performance practices, it does show both the kind of ornamentation and its sheer quantity to be particular to the Italian style; operatic vocal ornamentation of the time met with the same type of criticism. Some half a century later Rousseau's remarks (p. 86) indicate that the pressure to play with restraint and good taste and the sharp condemnation of the *Suonatoroni* (p. 88) had taken effect. The large amount of evidence found in Italian treatises and in musical sources explains in detail when and where it is appropriate to make divisions in the bass line demonstrating that this was, and is, a most refined art. Indications on how to simplify complex bass lines as well as how to ornament simple ones give the performer much scope for reinterpreting the composer's bass line in the manner most appropriate for the instrument and the occasion.

Extracting a Simple Bass Line

It has been seen (p. 39) how two bass lines were often played together, one simple harmonic version and the same bass with divisions. The demise of examples of two bass lines in printed music of the mid and late 1600s coincides with the emergence

---

49   Roma N.1, *Regole*, folio 65 v.
50   Pierre Bonnet, *Histoire de la musique, et de ses effets* (Paris, 1715).
51   Benedetto Marcello, *Il teatro alla moda* (Venice, 1720).

of written instructions on how to create both a simplification of a complex bass and on how to make divisions on a simple bass.

Penna and Bismantova write about this separation of the bass line and the difference between the simple version, a basso continuo, and what they define as a *basso cantante*, a more complex singing bass.[52] Bismantova explains how to extract a basso continuo line from a fast-moving bass: 'À più Bassi; il Continuo, si caverà dal più inferiore. Sè il Basso Cantante; farà movimenti in questo modo quà di sotto: [Example 4.60a] Il Basso Continuo; si farà in questo modo quà di sotto: [Example 4.60b]' ['When there is more than one bass, the continuo will be taken from the lowest; if the *basso cantante* moves like this: [Example 4.60a] The basso continuo will be made like this: [Example 4.60b]'].

Example 4.60a B. Bismantova, *Compendio musicale***, p. 59**

Example 4.60b B. Bismantova, *Compendio musicale***, p. 59**

Penna writes:

Si avverta, che quando il Basso Cantante farà tirate di note nere come di semiminime, ò Crome, ò Semicrome ascendenti, ò discendenti per grado, e ancora per salti purchè li salti non siano dissonanti; bastarà, che il Basso Continuo sia scritto con le note consonanti, che tenghino il valore di tutte quelle note nere.

[Note that when the *basso cantante* has run of black notes, be these crotchets, quavers or semiquavers, ascending or descending by step, or by leap (as long as those leaps are not dissonant), it will be sufficient for the basso continuo to be written out of the consonant notes, which hold the value of all those black notes.]

The examples Penna gives are identical to those given by Bismantova, as is often the case between these two authors. Both authors talk of the separation of the bass line and its treatment in those parts of their books dedicated to composition not to basso continuo. Only a short chapter, in both cases, deals with this quite fundamental aspect of treatment of the bass line, confirming that this was

---

[52] Penna, *Li primi albori musicali*, book 2, pp. 139–40; Bismantova, *Compendio musicale*, p. 59.

already a recognized and familiar practice. By the beginning of the 1700s basso continuo treatises actually started to describe how performers should make their own *basso cantante*.

Divisions of the Bass Line

The art of divisions in the accompanying bass line is not discussed in many Italian treatises, but two of the sources in which it is discussed are very detailed. These are the anonymous manuscript Roma N.1 and Francesco Gasparini's *L'armonico pratico*. Roma N.1 is generally in favour of divisions but Gasparini does not approve the practice, though he does teach how divisions ought to be played in the hope that they will be used wisely to turn a piece into something more beautiful and not as a means of drawing attention to the instrumentalist's virtuosity; French complaints evidently were not wholly unfounded nor the abuses left undeplored.

Chapter XVI of Roma N.1, 'Che sia diminutione' explains the principles of playing divisions:

> Diminuitione è quando per essempio ad'una nota che voglia mezza battuta si voglia fare qualche abbellimento per il quale si diminuisce il valore di detta nota, e si fanno figure minori consistenti nel valore di detta nota, e si posso[no] fare tanto ascendendo quanto descendendo. [Example 4.61] Si diminuisce ancora il salto di 3.a tanto ascendendo, quanto descendendo. [Example 4.62]

> [Division occurs when, for example, to a note that lasts half a bar, one wishes to add some ornament that will diminish the value of this note, and smaller figures are made in accordance with the value of this note; these [divisions] can be done ascending and descending. [Example 4.61] A leap of a third can also be diminished, both ascending or descending. [Example 4.62]]

Example 4.61   Roma N.1, *Regole per accompagnar sopra la parte*, folio 38v

Example 4.62   Roma N.1, *Regole per accompagnar sopra la parte*, folio 38v

The anonymous author emphasizes that the 're-composition' of the bass line should not interfere with the structure of the piece; a simple cadence should not form consecutive fifths or octaves with the parts above, and the accompanist should not change the bass line other than in a desirable place, for instance where the parts above move in contrary motion to the bass (Example 4.63). Examples of how to diminish each interval are given, ascending and descending: thirds, as in Example 4.62; fourths in Example 4.64; and fifths in Example 4.65.

Example 4.63   **Roma N.1,** *Regole per accompagnar sopra la parte*, **folio 41**

Example 4.64   **Roma N.1,** *Regole per accompagnar sopra la parte*, **folio 39**

Example 4.65   **Roma N.1,** *Regole per accompagnar sopra la parte*, **folio 39**

Emphasis is again placed on the importance of not playing divisions which would result in consecutive fifths; an example is given of an incorrect division (Example 4.66). Bass lines such as this should be avoided. The author specifies that a good division should return to the main note when making divisions of an interval of a second, third, fourth or fifth (as in example 4.61); whereas an upward leap of a sixth can only be diminished if turned into a downward leap of a third, and a downward leap of a sixth can only be diminished as an upward third

(Example 4.67). Similarly, sevenths can only be diminished by inversion (Example 4.68), and the author states that octaves can only be diminished with a semiquaver scale (Example 4.69). Cadence points can also be diminished (Example 4.70).

Example 4.66   Roma N.1, *Regole per accompagnar sopra la parte,* **folio 41**

Example 4.67   Roma N.1, *Regole per accompagnar sopra la parte,* **folio 41v**

Example 4.68   Roma N.1, *Regole per accompagnar sopra la parte,* **folio 41v**

Example 4.69   Roma N.1, *Regole per accompagnar sopra la parte,* **folio 41v**

Example 4.70   Roma N.1, *Regole per accompagnar sopra la parte,* **folio 42**

Example 4.71 shows further divisions with semiquavers. These are not in themselves divisions of the quaver examples above; they are further, more complicated types of division of the original bass.

Example 4.71   Roma N.1, *Regole per accompagnar sopra la parte,* **folio 42, 42v**

Divisions on the organ The organ is considered differently from the harpsichord and lutes (see p. 83); Roma N.1 tells the organist to avoid making divisions unless it is possible to play the original basso continuo line on pedals.

> Le diminuitioni dell'Organo non sono laudabili perchè si guasta il fondamento della musica movendosi il basso come cavo di tutta l'armonia mà tenendovi il pedale si potranno fare. Nel Cembalo che riescerà più moto per havere il mantenimento dell'armonia, si potranno concedere.

> [Divisions on the organ are not advisable because the music's foundation is spoiled when the bass moves, as the harmony becomes empty; but if the pedal is held, then it will be possible to play them. On the harpsichord, which will need more movement to maintain the harmony, they are allowed.]

Given the florid nature of some of the solo music for organ it is worth considering whether organists of the time would have respected this viewpoint; certainly the solo repertoire, just as with the harpsichord, takes into account the various stylistic ways in which the composers/performers reflected the taste of their time in devising ornamental figurations, as well as their ability to absorb them into their general compositional – and thus implicitly their actual – performing practice. A particularly florid style of writing is found, for example, in Josepho Antonio Paganelli: *XXX ariae pro organo et cembalo* (1756), which often contains pertinent examples of figurations associated with the galante style. Even more indicative is the eighteenth-century Italian repertoire for two or more organs, for example the works by Luchinetti, Piazza and Terreni, showing the effectiveness of written-out 'broken chord' figurations (Luchinetti), or a whole host of galante decorative devices (Terreni).[53]

Burney complains:

> It were to be wished that [the organist] and his colleagues would accompany the voices and instruments, which are good and well worth hearing, with the Choir Organs [2nd manuals] only, as we do in England; for, other wise, nothing *but* the organs can be heard; they are, indeed, fine toned instruments, but so powerful as to render all the rest of the performance useless.[54]

Added ornamentation would have confused the sound even further.

Discretion in divisions It is in Chapter XI of *L'armonico pratico*, 'Del diminuire, o rifiorire il Fondamento', that Gasparini makes it clear how strongly he disapproves of the possible results of diminishing the bass line on any instrument: 'Il diminuire il proprio basso io non l'approvo, perchè si può facilmente uscire, allontanandosi

---

53   Gerald Gifford, personal communication.
54   Charles Burney, *Travels* I, p. 104, quoted in Peter Williams, *The European Organ 1450–1850* (London, 1966), p. 205.

dall'intenzione dell'Autore, dal buon gusto della Composizione, e offender il Cantante' ['I do not approve of divisions on one's bass, because it is easy to part from the author's intention and the *buon gusto* of the composition, offending the singer']. For Gasparini to state his views so baldly on divisions further suggests the practice was used widely and, if resulting in the effects described by Bonnet and Marcello, greatly misused.

Gasparini's divisions (Example 4.72–4.72e) differ from those of Roma N.1: 'Riflettendo, che questo è un'arpeggio cavato dalle proprie Consonanze, sarà facile allo Studioso prenderne l'uso, ma con giudicio' ['Considering that this is an arpeggio formed from its own consonances, it will be easy for the scholar to undertake its use, but judiciously']. Gasparini's examples do consist of an 'arpeggio formed from its own consonances'; the bass is broken but never strays from the harmonies implied by the chord. Roma N.1 shows how to recompose the bass according to the rules of composition. Gasparini's objection to the charmless confusion divisions can create within a piece led him to print his own divisions of the bass in his *Cantate da camera* op. 1, discussed later (pp. 123–5).

Example 4.72   F. Gasparini, *L'armonico pratico*, pp. 105–7

Altro modo

Example 4.72a F. Gasparini, *L'armonico pratico*, pp. 105–7

In un tempo più andante

Example 4.72b F. Gasparini, *L'armonico pratico*, pp. 105–7

In tripla, o altra Proporzione

Example 4.72c F. Gasparini, *L'armonico pratico*, pp. 105–7

Altro modo

Example 4.72d F. Gasparini, *L'armonico pratico*, pp. 105–7

Essendo il tempo più veloce

Example 4.72e F. Gasparini, *L'armonico pratico*, pp. 105–7

Diminished bass lines without commentary As well as these texts with musical examples there are also manuscript examples of diminished bass lines which have no commentary. The practice was documented from as early as the second half of the 1600s; for the lute, MS C311 of the Biblioteca Estense in Modena covers many ways of making divisions at cadence points.[55] In the Biblioteca di San Piero a Majella in Naples, a manuscript of Rocco Greco not specifically for any instrument gives examples of diminished bass lines, again with no commentary (Example 4.73).[56]

---

[55]   MS C311 (IMOe).
[56]   MS 33-2-3 (INc).

Example 4.73   R. Greco, INc (MS 33-2-3)

Right-hand Realizations

Together with this more elaborate treatment of the bass line, right-hand realizations begin to be more clearly documented and discussed in treatises from the beginning of the eighteenth century.

Tessitura of the right hand By tessitura, the range in which the right hand is playing is meant. Theorists and composers all advise keeping the realization in the same range as the singer, especially at cadences, echoing the teachings of Viadana and the authors of the previous century (p. 53). Penna comments:[57]

> Che l' Organista habbi l' occhio aperto, e pronto, non solo alla sua parte, mà ancora alla parte Cantante, collocatevi sopra, per accompagnarla con li tasti, corrispondenti alla voce, per Esempio se sarà il Soprano, tocchi li Soprani, se sarà il Contralto, suoni li tasti dell' Alto, procurando di esser presto à toccar il tasto per dar la voce al Cantore. [Example 4.74a] Che non potendo accompagnare tutte le Note cantanti, prenda solamente le Consonanze, ò almeno la prima e ultima del battere, e la prima e ultima del levar di mano, lasciando le altre come l' Esempio. [Example 4.74b]

> [The organist's eyes should be open and alert, not only to their part, but also to the part that is singing, which is placed above, so that it may be accompanied with the keys that correspond to the voice; for example, if soprano, then play in the soprano [register], if alto, play the keys of the alto; try to be quick in touching the keys in order to give voice [that is, notes] to the singer. [Example 4.74a] If it is not possible to accompany [play] all the notes that are being sung, only the consonances should be played, or at least the first and the last of the downbeat and the first and last of the upbeat, leaving the others, as in the example. [Example 4.74b]]

Just as in the 1600s, the accompanist should keep the realization of the bass in the same register as the voice that is singing. Bismantova comments similarly:[58]

> Quando s'accompagnano le Compositioni, à Voce Sola; che l' Organista habbi l'occhio pronto, non solo alla sua parte; mà anco alla parte di sopra del Cantore; e nel suonare sij presto, à toccare li Tasti che sono corrispondenti alla voce di detto Cantore; acciò il

---

[57]   Penna, *Li primi albori musicali*, p. 184.
[58]   Bismantova, *Compendio musicale*, pp. 81–2.

Example 4.74a L. Penna, *Li primi albori, Dell'accompagnare le composizioni a voce sola,* **p. 184**

Example 4.74b L. Penna, *Li primi albori, Dell'accompagnare le composizioni a voce sola,* **p. 184**

Cantante possi pigliar la voce; e sè à caso, non si potesse accompagnare tutte le note cantanti; si prenda solamente le Consonanze; ò almeno la prima del battere, e la prima del levare di mano, lasciando le altre.

[When accompanying compositions for one voice, the organist must be alert not only to his own part, but also to the part of the singer, placed above; and when playing he must be quick to touch those keys that correspond to the voice of the singer, so that the singer may get his notes. If, by chance, it is not possible to accompany all the sung notes, one must play only the consonances, or at least the first downbeat and the first upbeat, leaving the others.]

Pasquini agrees that the accompaniment should be in the same register as the voice accompanied: 'Non coprir la parte che canta; cioè se canta il soprano fare la cadenza in detto Soprano, e toccar le corde del soprano, e se canta il contralto, fare il simile' ['Do not cover [play above] the part which is singing; that is, if the soprano is singing, play the cadence in the soprano [register], and play the notes of the soprano; if an alto is singing, do the same'].[59] Yet Roma N.1 introduces, although does not recommend, the possibility of playing a third above the vocal line: 'L'accompagnamento con la 3.a superiore è biasmato, volendo alcuni, che non si superi la parte che canta, essendo soprano; io però mi rimetto al buon gusto di chi suona' ['Accompanying a third above is not recommended, as some

---

[59]   Bernardo Pasquini, *Regole* (IBc, D.138), p. 2.

wish that [the accompaniment] should not exceed the part that is singing, if this is a soprano; however, I leave it up to the good taste of the player'].

The advantage of playing in the register of the singer is that should they lose their note it can be given to them discreetly, skilfully woven into the right-hand realization. To play the right-hand realization in the same register as the soprano voice results in a very high-profile, exposed accompaniment; the balance with the voice being accompanied is more delicate. To keep low when accompanying low instruments and voices is instinctive and results in a soft accompaniment that is supportive without drawing attention to itself. In practice, it is most interesting of all if the tessitura of the realization changes according to what is being accompanied and the effect that is desired rather than strict adherance to the soloist's range.

Right-hand Realization during Rests in the Vocal Part

Penna merely encourages players to imitate the motifs that have just been sung as soon as the voice finishes: 'Che nelli Ritornelli, ò Pause, poste per riposo del Cantante, l'Organista suoni alquanto di suo Capriccio, imitando l'Arietta, ò altro allegro, cantato di fresco' ['In the refrains, or pauses, introduced [to allow] the singer to rest, the organist should play as he chooses, imitating the *arietta*, or other immediately preceding motif'].[60] Roma N.1 talks of the right-hand realization in relation to the bass as well as to the part being accompanied: 'Si potranno farsi alcuni piccole diminuitioni tanto nel soprano, quanto nel basso, come: [Example 4.75]' ['Some little diminutions can be played in the soprano as well as in the bass, such as: [Example 4.75]']. Note the D in the second chord, an example of a long *acciaccatura*.

Example 4.75   Roma N.1, *Regole per accompagnar sopra la parte*, folio 42v

---

[60]   Penna, *Li primi albori musicali*, p. 185.

Here the continuo player is recomposing the bass line in the left hand and in the right hand playing imitations of the composer's vocal line, and further elaborating it; this skill will have been developed by study of the *Partimenti* (see p. 76). When developing this improvisatory technique through the study of *Partimenti*, however, the harpsichordist needed only to take into account the relationship between the right hand and the written bass line; when accompanying, melodic improvisation would have been restricted mainly to when the voice was silent. It is for this reason that a wholly composed accompaniment such as *Da sventura à sventura* (p. 81) is not representative of basso continuo practice in performance.

Gasparini considers right-hand realizations in Chapter X, 'Del diminuire, abbellire, o rifiorire gli accompagnamenti' of *L'armonico pratico*. In his examples right-hand decorations are given above formulaic bass lines; just as in the *regole d'accompagnamento*, different movements of the bass are exemplified: ascending, descending, moving by step and by leap, and cadences (Example 4.76). On the last cadence, note the trill between the E and D in the inner voices written above the figures.

Example 4.76   F. Gasparini, *L'armonico pratico*, p. 98 (the first two examples)

Gasparini explains that the chords indicated by the figures are to be played in the left hand, leaving the right hand free to realize the decorations: 'Si procuri dunque osservando questi esempi di dar le Consonanze necessarie con la mano sinistra, e con la destra sonar la parte superiore, come quì si dimostra' ['Make sure then, when observing these examples, to give the necessary consonances with the left hand, and with the right to play the upper part, as shown here'].

The practice of playing the chords in the left hand and improvising in the right, therefore using the left hand as the continuo and the right hand as the melodic line, is a practice used in solo music as well as in continuo realization; Alessandro Scarlatti's 'Varie Introduttioni per sonare, e mettersi in tono delle Composizioni' is written in such a fashion and bears the indication 'qui la consonanza piena colla mano sinistra' ['play full consonances with the left hand'] (Example 4.77).

Varie Introduttioni per sonare, e mettersi in tono delle Composizioni

Qui la consonanza piena colla mano sinistra

Example 4.77   A. Scarlatti, GBLbl, Add. 14244, folio 46v

Taste and awareness Gasparini refers the reader of *L'armonico pratico* to his *Cantate da camera* for examples of how to diminish the bass with taste and awareness;[61] furthermore, the *Cantate* also include examples of right-hand realizations where the voice rests, just as he had described in his theoretical work. In the Preface he writes:

> Troverete in alcune arie dui Bassi uno per comodo, ò facilità di accompagnare; essendo stato necessario anche accomodarsi alla Stampa, che non hà potuto totalmente dimostrar la mia intenzione. Però dove si trovano sopra il Basso alcune chiavi di Canto,

---

61   Francesco Gasparini, *Cantate da camera a voce sola, opera prima* (Rome, 1695).

ò Violino si soneranno con la mano destra in forma d'intavolatura. Ivi potranno ancora sodisfarsi l'Arcileuto, e Violoncello.

[In some arias you will find two basses, one for convenience and ease of accompaniment; apart from printing difficulties which have prevented me from fully showing my intention. But where, over the bass, a soprano clef or a violin clef have been placed, these are to be played with the right hand in the form of *intavolatura*. These can be of use also to the archlute and the cello.]

The second aria of the fourth cantata, *Dove sei dove t'ascondi* has right-hand realizations where the voice is not singing and, where the voice does enter, the bass line separates into two lines, one simple bass and the other diminished, exactly as Gasparini explains in *L'armonico pratico* (Example 4.78). Clearly in the parts where the right hand is written out, chords are intended to be played in the left hand, and where the left hand has divisions, chords are intended in the right hand.

Example 4.78   F. Gasparini, *Cantate da camera a voce sola*, 'Dove sei dove t'ascondi'

Gasparini also exemplifies right-hand realizations in the manuscript cantata *Andate ò miei sospiri* (Example 4.79);[62] that it should be found in a musical manuscript is significant as it shows that the examples in *L'armonico pratico* and in his *Cantate da camera* are not purely didactic cross-references.

Example 4.79   **F. Gasparini, *Andate ò miei sospiri*, Biblioteca del Conservatorio di Musica S. Pietro a Majella di Napoli (MS 6.3.5)**

Gasparini wrote *Andate ò miei sospiri* for Alessandro Scarlatti, a recipient who certainly would not have needed Gasparini's suggestions for right-hand improvisations; Gasparini evidently considered right-hand, melodic realizations as an integral part of his compositions and of basso continuo accompaniment, which explains why, in Chapter X of *L'armonico pratico*, he described possible realizations in such detail.

Divisions on other continuo instruments Gasparini's reference to cello and archlute (p. 124) does not imply that it was necessary for these two bass lines to be played simultaneously. Roma N.1 clarifies: 'A chi piacerà le diminuitioni in semicrome potrà valersi delle precedenti; quali potranno servire anco per il leuto, et altri instromenti' ['Those who like divisions in semiquavers will be able to use the former [examples], which can also be of use to the lute and other instruments'], indicating that divisions are appropriate also for lutenists and cellists. If two bass instruments are present then it is possible for both bass lines to be played, but it should not be assumed that the harpsichordist specifically should play the *basso cantabile*; the mention of lutes and cellos indicates that this practice can be emulated on other instruments as well – indeed it encourages the writing of *bassi cantabili* that lend themselves to melody instruments.

In the case of the cantata *Dove sei, dove t'ascondi*, it is possible for the harpsichord alone to play both the simple and, when it occurs, more elaborate

---

62   Francesco Gasparini, *Andate ò miei sospiri* (INc, MS 6.3.5).

bass line, thus making the bass line more sustained. This subtler alteration to the bass line renders it more idiomatic to the harpsichord; it is a further technique used to keep the sound of the instrument alive.

Gasparini closes Chapter X by summarizing the relationship between the *regole d'accompagnamento* and divisions in the left and/or the right hand:

> E con simil maniera si può ricercar ogni sorte d'accompagnamento ... Si dovrà però avvertire con simili diminuizioni, o vogliamo dir fioretti, di non confonder il Cantore, sfuggendo d'incontrarsi in far l'istesso passo, o maniera, che potesse fare il medesimo. Come ancora non si deve mai suonare ad notam quello, che fa la parte, che canta, o altra parte superiore Composta per violino eccetera mentre basta, che nel corpo dell'Armonia vi si trovi quella Consonanza, o Dissonanza, che sarà composta, o richiesta dal fondamento, *conforme alle regole dell'accompagnamento* [emphasis added].

> [And in a similar fashion one can try out any kind of accompaniment ... However, one should be careful with such divisions, or shall we say embellishments, not to confuse the singer, avoiding adopting the same step, or manner [i.e. the same notes] that the singer himself might do. And again one should never play the same notes as the singer's part or any higher part composed for violin etcetera, as it suffices for the body of the harmony to contain that consonance, or dissonance, which will be formed, or required by the bass, *in conformity with the rules of accompaniment*.]

The conservatism of Gasparini's conclusion is somewhat at odds with his detailed explanations and examples of how – always with good taste – to play precisely what here he advises against. The continuo player should play 'the body of harmony with the consonances or dissonances required by the bass, conforming to the rules of accompaniment'; divisions are not intended when any other part is playing, but only where the other parts are silent; then melodic lines are improvised above the bass line, playing chords with the left hand and improvising in the right.

Chapter 5

The End of Basso Continuo Creativity

Continuo Post-1750

The rules set out at the beginning of the 1700s embody the evolution of basso continuo accompaniment; treatises written in the second half of the 1700s show little development or change from half a century earlier. The style was fully formed and formulated if, at times, the practice was over-florid; Gasparini was still used as one of the main texts on the subject – first published in 1708, it was reprinted eight times, with the last publication at the beginning of the nineteenth century.[1]

Throughout the period 1600–1770 there had been a tension between the idea of the harmonic accompaniment following the *regole d'accompagnamento* and guided by the soloist's interpretation, and the keyboard player's predilection for compositional improvised melodic right-hand realization and recomposing the bass in the left hand. In 1754, Geminiani published in *The Art of Accompaniment*:

> Some perhaps will be surprized to find so little Resemblance between this Book, and those which have been published by others, upon the same Subject. Had any, or all of those Books together, contained compleat Directions for the just Performance of Thorough Bass, I should not have offered mine to the Publick. But I will take upon me to say, that it is impossible to arrive at the just Performance of Thorough Bass, by the Help of any, or all of the Books hitherto published.[2]

His treatise is divided into two parts; in the first he explains, with few words but many formulaic musical examples, every chord and its inversion and how these should follow one another in order to produce the most beautiful melodic outline in the accompaniment, while still providing harmonic support. The resulting accompaniment is that of the *regole d'accompagnamento*; the skill of the continuo player consists in varying the character of the chords in accordance with what is being accompanied. In the second part of the treatise Geminiani gives examples of right-hand realizations with melodic flourishes, reminiscent of what Gasparini had published some half a century earlier (p. 122); these are clearly

---

[1]   As Tagliavini reports in '*L'armonico pratico al cimbalo*, lettura critica', Gasparini's treatise was printed in Venice in 1708, with subsequent reprints in 1715, 1729, 1745, 1754, 1764; in Bologna it was reprinted in 1713 and 1722. Its last reprint before modern times was in 1802, in Venice.

[2]   Geminiani, *The Art of Accompaniment, part the first* (London, 1754), 'Preface'.

derived from the practice of *Partimenti* and the right-hand writing is composed in accordance with the movement of the bass rather than reacting to the part that is being accompanied. This treatise sums up and explains these two strands of accompanying, chordally and melodically; in the Introduction to the second part of this treatise, Geminiani explains how the two should be combined in practice, putting forward this answer to critics of accompaniment in the Italian manner:

> It will perhaps be said, that the following Examples are arbitrary Compositions upon the Bass; and it may be asked how this arbitrary Manner of accompanying can agree with the Intention and Stile of all sorts of Compositions. Moreover a fine Singer or Player, when he finds himself accompanied in this Manner, will perhaps complain that he is interrupted, and the Beauties of his Performance thereby obscured, and deprived of their Effect. To this I answer, That a good Accompanyer ought to possess the Faculty of playing all sorts of Basses, in different Manners; so as to be able, on proper Occasions, to enliven the Composition, and delight the Singer or Player. But he is to exercise this Faculty with Judgment, Taste, and Discretion, agreeable to the Stile of the Composition, and the Manner and Intention of the Performer. If an Accompanyer thinks of nothing else but the satisfying his own Whim and Caprice, he may perhaps be said to play well, but will certainly be said to accompany ill.

By following Geminiani's method the harpsichordist would gain the skills needed to improvise well above the bass; the finest style of continuo playing, as Geminiani reiterates, was a combination of these improvisatory skills and the *regole d'accompagnamento*, which would have been used to react to the part that was being accompanied – a pre-eminent purpose and strength of basso continuo.

Ending Improvisation in Continuo Performance

Indications from the composer to the continuo player in both printed and manuscript sources became more explicit towards the second half of the eighteenth century, showing how composers were beginning to restrict the continuo player's liberty in the interpretation of the score. In printed music, Francesco Maria Veracini was one of the first Italian composers to take the greatest care over exactly what the continuo was playing. In his *Sonate Accademiche* of 1744, he specifies precisely where chords should be placed and where the continuo should play *tasto solo*, giving these instructions in his Introduction:

> S. Significa Nota Sola; cio è senza più ribatterla finche passi tutto il tempo del di lei valore. Tal segno serve al Cimbalo Tiorba e Liuto. L'Organo, e gl'altri strumenti, che possono devono sostenerla.

S significa Sole; cioè tutte quelle Note, che succedono a detto segno, si devono sonare sul Cimbalo con tasto solo, finche si trovino Le Segnature; indi accompagnarle al solito.[3]

[*S*. means a single note – it should not be restruck until the whole value of the note has passed. This sign serves for the harpsichord, theorbo and lute. The organ, and other instruments that can, must sustain it.

S means *tasto solo* – that is, all those notes that follow this sign should be played *tasto solo* by the harpsichord, for as long as the sign is there, then accompany as usual.]

This is an example of a most controlled use of continuo, where the presence of more or fewer notes in the chords is marked by the composer directly on the score.

For orchestral music, an example of outstanding attention to detail in the continuo player's part is found in the manuscript score of Marc'Antonio Ziani's serenata *La Flora*.[4] There are many occasions where, in the bass part, the indication *pochi tasti* appears – most often when accompanying a solo instrument or voice within an orchestral aria – an explicit indication that the harpsichord should play few notes, therefore making the realization insubstantial yet without renouncing the sound of the harpsichord completely (Example 5.1).

The End of the Performance of Basso Continuo

The teaching of figured bass carried on into the nineteenth century, but the relationship with style in the realization of the bass became more and more tenuous as bass lines with only figures were becoming rarer and editorial realizations of figured basses appeared.[5] Treatises published at this time were studies on harmony without reference to performance;[6] some continue to be used now for the teaching of harmony.

---

3   Francesco Maria Veracini, *Sonate accademiche a violino solo e basso* (London and Florence, 1744).

4   Marc'Antonio Ziani, *La Flora* (IVnm, cl. 4, n.572, 9852).

5   See Ausilia Magaudda and Danilo Costantini, 'Tradizione ottocentesca nella realizzazione dei bassi nei salmi di Benedetto Marcello' in Claudio Madricardo and Franco Rossi (eds), *Benedetto Marcello: la sua opera e il suo tempo. Atti del Convegno internazionale, Venezia, 15–17 dicembre 1986* (Florence, 1988), pp. 425–49 for a discussion of these first editorial realizations of the nineteenth century.

6   See Andrea Basili, *Musica universale armonico pratica ... per i suonatori di Grave Cembalo, ed Organo* (Venice, 1775); Fedele Fenaroli, *Regole musicali per li principianti di cembalo nel sonar co i numeri* (Naples, 1775); Giuseppe Livereziani, *Grammatica della Musica ... con regole per ben cantare e suonare il cembalo* (Rome, 1797); Giovanni Paisiello, *Regole per bene accompagnare il partimento, o sia il basso fondamentale sopra il cembalo* (St Petersburg, 1782); Vincenzo Panerai, *Principi di musica ... e prime regole del cimbalo* (Florence, 1780); Johann Michel Pfeiffer, *La bambina al cembalo ... per apprendere a ben suonare ed accompagnare sopra il clavicembalo o fortepiano* (Venice, 1785); Pellegrino Tomeoni, *Regole pratiche per accompagnare il basso continuo* (Florence, 1795).

Example 5.1   M.A. Ziani, *La Flora*, Biblioteca Nazionale Marciana, Venezia (cod.It.IV, 572 (=9852))

Manfredini, writing as late as 1775, is author of one the last treatises specifically on continuo performance;[7] he conforms completely to the teachings of the beginning of the century, explaining stylistic matters particularly lucidly and comprehensively. He sums up the *regole d'accompagnamento* perfectly, supplying all the *regole* with examples of their realization – he is the first and only writer to do this. As basso continuo accompaniment falls into disuse, his treatise articulates clearly its versatility and re-emphasizes the responsibility of the accompanist to regulate the number of notes placed in a chord in accordance with what is being accompanied and where. The same things were being said in the 1600s, in the first explanatory introductions to operas, but never had they been explained so fully and demanded so directly. In his 'Osservazioni per bene accompagnare' Manfredini writes:

> Deve dunque chi accompagna sonare il Basso come sta scritto, e non riempire gli Accordi, né raddoppiarli colla mano sinistra, se non quando vi ha bisogno di far molto rumore; come per esempio in una grande Orchestra, o in una Musica Ecclesiastica a più Cori;

---

[7]   Manfredini, *Regole armoniche*.

[The person accompanying must play the bass as it is written, and not fill out the chords, or double them with the left hand, other than when much sound is needed; for example in a large orchestra, or in sacred music with many voices;]

Although the principles he describes are in keeping with earlier writing and practice he goes on to recommend a poverty-striken mode of accompaniment for the solo voice wholly unlike that advised by Gasparini and his contemporaries: 'ma accompagnando un Cantante solo, o un sol Sonatore, deve colla sinistra mano eseguire il Basso solo, o al più al più aggiugnergli l'Ottava, e con la destra, far poca Armonia' ['but when accompanying just one singer, or just one player, with the left hand one must play only the bass line, or at the very most add the octave to it, and play limited harmony with the right hand'].

This reflects the growing trend towards emphasis on the solo voice and simple, non-intrusive accompaniment; or to wholly composed accompaniments. By the 1770s, composers ceased to call for improvisation and preferred to compose their own accompaniments to form an integral part of the composition and interact with the solo part in accordance with their taste. No longer was it left to the performer to judge how to vary the accompaniment; basso continuo was superseded by other systems of notation for accompaniments that fulfilled different stylistic needs. Changes in instruments meant that it was no longer necessary for the performer to adapt the bass line to the instrument being played, as harpsichords, lutes and theorboes were no longer used; improvisatory techniques such as *arpeggi* and *acciaccature*, essential for keeping the sound of these instruments alive, were no longer appropriate as new instruments responded with dynamics and expression from a fully written-out part.

Changes in style, changes in taste, new instruments and the general aesthetics of the period had brought basso continuo accompaniment into being. It took half a century for basso continuo to be formalized and adopted as the best way to accompany; for almost two centuries it continued to transform under the fingers of its performers, until composers took control of the markings of versatility in accompaniment.

Select Bibliography

Agazzari, A. *Copia d'una lettera*, in A. Banchieri, *Conclusioni nel suono dell'organo, op. XX* (Bologna, 1609).

Agazzari, A. *Del sonare sopra 'l basso con tutti li stromenti e dell'uso loro nel conserto* (Siena, 1607). Facsimile reprint (Bologna, 1985).

Agazzari, A. *Sacrae cantiones* (Venice, 1608).

Allegri, L. *Il primo libro delle musiche* (Venice, 1618).

dell'Antonio, A. 'La maniera di cantare con affetti cantabili: The Seconda Prattica and Instrumental music'. Appendix in *Syntax, Form and Genre in Sonatas and Canzonas 1621–1635* (Lucca, 1997).

Banchieri, A. *Cartella musicale nel canto figurato fermo e contrapunto* (Venice, 1614).

Banchieri, A. *Conclusioni nel suono dell'organo* (Bologna, 1609).

Banchieri, A. *Dialogo musicale*, in *L'organo suonarino* (Venice, 1605). Facsimile reprint (Bologna, 1978).

Banchieri, A. *Gemelli armonici* (Venice, 1609).

Banchieri, A. *Lettere armoniche* (Bologna, 1630).

Banchieri, A. *L'organo suonarino* (Bologna, 1605).

Barbarino, B. *Il secondo libro de madrigali de diversi autori … per cantare sopra il chitarrone ò tiorba, clavicembalo, ò altri stromenti da una voce sola* (Venice, 1607).

Barbieri, P. 'Conflitti di intonazione tra cembalo, liuti e archi nel 'concerto' italiano del seicento', *Studi Corelliani IV, Quaderni della Rivista Italiana di Musicologia* (1986).

Basili, A. *Musica universale armonico pratica … per i suonatori di Grave Cembalo, ed Organo* (Venice, 1775).

Bianciardi, F. *Breve regola per imparar' a sonare sopra il basso* (Siena, 1607).

Bianconi, L. *Il seicento* (Turin, 1991).

Bismantova, B. *Compendio musicale* (Ferrara, 1677). Facsimile reprint (Florence, 1978).

Bonini, S. *Madrigali e canzonette spirituali* (Florence, 1607).

Bonini, S. *Prima parte de' discorsi e regole sovra la musica*, ed. L.G. Luisi (Cremona, 1975).

Bonnet, P. *Histoire de la musique, et de ses effets* (Paris, 1715).

Bossinensis, F. (Franjo Bosanac). *Tenori e contrabbassi intabulati col sopran in canto figurato per cantar e sonar col lauto* (Libro primo, Venice, 1509 and Libro secondo, Fossombrone, 1511).

Bottrigari, E. *Il desiderio, o vero de' concerti di varij strumenti musicali* (Venice, 1594).

Brunetti, G. *Salmi intieri concertati à 5 e 6* (Venice, 1625).

Bruschi, A.F. *Regole per il contrapunto, e per l'accompagnatura del basso continuo compendiate, e dilucidate da Antonio Filippo Bruschi Fiorentino* (Lucca, 1711).

Burney, C. *The present state of Music in France and Italy*, (London, 1771). Facsimile reprint (London, 2002).

Caccini, G. *Le nuove musiche* (Florence, 1601). Facsimile reprint (Florence, 1983).

Caccini, G. *L'Euridice* (Florence, 1600). Facsimile reprint (Bologna, 1976).

dalla Casa, F. *Regole di musica, ed anco le regole per accompagnare sopra la parte per suonare il basso continuo, & per l'arcileuto francese, e per la tiorba* (Bologna, 1759).

Castaldi, B. *Capricci a due strumenti cioè tiorba e tiorbino* (Modena, 1622).

Castiglione, B. *Il libro del Cortegiano* (Florence, 1528).

de' Cavalieri, E. *Rappresentazione di Anima, et di Corpo* (Rome, 1600). Facsimile reprint (Bologna, 1987).

Cavalli, A. 'Le cantate opera prima di Francesco Gasparini', *Chigiana*, vol. 25 (1968), pp. 54–68.

Cerreto, S. *Della prattica musica vocale e strumentale* (Naples, 1601).

Cima, G. P. *Concerti Ecclesiastici, a' una, due, tre, quattro voci* (Milan, 1610).

Corradi, F. *Le Stravaganze d'Amore, a una, due e tre voci* (Venice, 1616).

Costantini, F. *Ghirlandetta amorosa, Arie, Madrigali, e Sonetti, di diversi ... autori, opera settima, libro primo* (Orvieto, 1621).

Dixon, G. 'Continuo Scoring in the Early Baroque: The Role of Bowed-bass Instruments', *Chelys*, vol. 15 (1986), pp. 38–53.

Doni, G.B. *Trattato della musica scenica*, in *De' trattati di musica*, ed. A.F. Gori (Florence, 1763).

Durante, E. and Martellotti, A. *Cronistoria del concerto* (Florence, 1989).

Fabbri, P. *Monteverdi* (Turin, 1985).

Fenaroli, F. *Regole musicali per li principianti di cembalo nel sonar co i numeri* (Naples, 1775).

Fenlon, I. and Haar, J. *The Italian Madrigal in the Early Sixteenth Century: Sources and Interpretation* (Cambridge, 1988).

Franzoni, A. *Concerti ecclesiastici a una, due, et a tre voci col basso continuo per l'organo* (Venice, 1611).

Frescobaldi, G. *Il Primo libro delle canzoni a una, due, tre, e quattro voci* (Rome, 1628).

Frescobaldi, G. *Primo Libro di Toccate e Partite d'Intavolatura di Cimbalo* (Rome, 1615). Facsimile reprint (Florence, 1980).

da Gagliano, M. *La Dafne* (Florence, 1608). Facsimile reprint (Bologna, 1987).

Galilei, V. *Fronimo dialogo di Vincenzo Galilei fiorentino* (Venice, 1568).

Gasparini, F. *Cantate da camera a voce sola, opera prima* (Rome, 1695). Facsimile reprint (Florence, 1984).

Gasparini, F. *L'armonico pratico al cimbalo* (Venice, 1708).

Gasparini, F. *L'armonico pratico al cimbalo*. Fourth impression, annotated by Padre Martini (Bologna, 1722).

Geminiani, F. *The Art of Accompaniment or A new and well digested method to learn to perform the Thorough Bass on the Harpsichord* (London, 1754). Facsimile reprint (Florence, 1990).

Giacobbi, G. *Prima parte dei salmi concertati a due, e più chori* (Venice, 1609).

Hill, J.W. 'Realized continuo accompaniments from Florence c. 1600', *Early Music*, vol. 11 (1983), pp. 194–208.

Horsley, I. 'Full and Short Scores in the Accompaniment of Italian Church Music in the Early Baroque', *Journal of the American Musicological Society*, vol. 30 (1977), pp. 466–99.

Kapsberger, J.H. *Libro primo di arie passeggiate à una voce con l'Intavolatura del Chitarrone* (Rome, 1612).

Kapsberger, J.H. *Libro primo di Villanelle* (Rome, 1610).

Kapsberger, J.H. *Libro terzo di Villanelle* (Rome, 1619).

Landi, S. *Il S. Alessio* (Rome, 1634).

Lindley, M. *Lutes, viols and temperaments* (Cambridge, 1984).

Livereziani, G. *Grammatica della Musica ... con regole per ben cantare e suonare il cembalo* (Roma, 1797).

Luzzaschi, L. *Madrigali per cantare et sonare a uno, e doi, e tre soprani* (Roma, 1601). Ed. A. Cavicchi (Brescia, 1965).

Manfredini, V. *Regole armoniche ... l'accompagnamento del basso sopra gli strumenti da tasto* (Bologna, 1775). Facsimile reprint (New York, 1966).

Mangsen, S. 'The Trio Sonata in pre-Corellian Prints: When Does 3 = 4?', *Performance Practice Review*, vol. 3 (1990), pp. 138–64.

Marcello, B. *Il teatro alla moda* (Venice, 1720).

Marcello, B. *Lettera familiare d'un accademico filarmonico et arcade discorsiva sopra un libro di duetti, terzetti e madrigali a più voci stampato in Venezia da Antonio Bortoli l'anno 1705* (Venice, ? after 1704).

Marini, B. *Scherzi e canzonette* (Parma, 1622).

Massaini, T. *Musica per cantare con l'organo ad una, due e tre voci* (Venice, 1607).

Materassi, M. 'Teoria e pratica del suonare sopra'l basso nel primo Seicento', *Il 'Fronimo'* (October 1979), pp. 24–32.

Mayer Brown, H. *Instrumental Music Printed before 1600; A Bibliography* (Cambridge, MA, 1965).

Mazzocchi, D. *La catena d'Adone* (Rome, 1626).

Mazzocchi, D. *Musiche Sacre, e morali a una, due e tre voci* (Rome, 1640).

Merula, T. *Il primo Libro delle Canzoni a quattro voci per sonre con ogni sorte di stromenti musicali* (Venice, 1615).

Milanuzzi, C. *Primo scherzo delle ariose vaghezze commode da cantarsi a voce sola nel clavicembalo, chitarrone, arpa doppia, e altro simile stromenti* (Venice, 1622).

Mompellio, F. 'Un certo ordine di procedere che non si può scrivere', *Scritti in onore di Luigi Ronga* (Milan and Naples, 1973).

Montesardo, G. *I lieti giorni di Napoli, concertini italiani in aria spagnuola a due, e tre voci con tutte le lettere dell'alfabeto della chitarra* (Naples, 1612).

Monteverdi, C. *Lettere, dediche e prefazioni / Claudio Monteverdi*, ed. Domenico De' Paoli (Rome, 1973).

Monteverdi, C. *L'Orfeo, Favola in Musica* (Venice, 1609).

Monteverdi, C. *Settimo Libro de Madrigali a 1, 2, 3, 4 e sei voci, con altri generi de canti* (Venice, 1619).

Monteverdi, C. *Vespro della Beata Vergine* (Venice, 1610). Facsimile reprint (Opglabbeek, 1992).

Nerici, L. *Storia della musica in Lucca* (Lucca, 1879). Facsimile reprint (Bologna, 1969).

Ortiz, D. *Tratado de glosas sobre clausulas y otros generos de puntos en la musica de violones* (Rome, 1553). Facsimile reprint (Florence, 1984).

Paisiello, G. *Regole per bene accompagnare il partimento, o sia il basso fondamentale sopra il cembalo* (St Petersburg, 1782).

Palisca, C. *The Florentine Camerata* (New Haven, CT, and London, 1989).

Panerai, V. *Principi di musica … e prime regole del cimbalo* (Florence, 1780).

Penna, L. *Li primi albori musicali* (Bologna, 1684). Facsimile reprint (Bologna, 1996).

Peri, J. *Le musiche sopra l'Euridice* (Florence, 1600). Facsimile reprint (Bologna, 1979).

Pfeiffer, J.M. *La bambina al cembalo … per apprendere a ben suonare ed accompagnare sopra il clavicembalo o fortepiano* (Venice, 1785).

Piccioni, G. *Concerti ecclesiastici … a una, a due, a tre, a quattro, a cinque, a sei, a sette, e a otto voci, con il suo Basso seguito per l'organo* (Venice, 1610).

Pirrotta, N. *Li due orfei; da Poliziano a Monteverdi* (Turin, 1975).

Porta, E. *Sacro convito musicale … a una, due, tre, quattro, cinque, e sei voci* (Venice, 1620).

Prizer, W. *Courtly Pastimes: The Frottole of Marchetto Cara*, ed. George Buelow, vol. 33, *Studies in Musicology* (Ann Arbor: UMI Research Press, 1980).

Puliaschi, G.D. *Musiche varie a una voce con il suo Basso continuo per sonare* (Rome, 1618).

Rognoni, D. *Canzoni à 4 e 8 voci* (Milan, 1605).

Rose, G. 'Agazzari and the improvising orchestra', *Journal of the American Musicological Society*, vol. 18 (1965), pp. 382–93.

Rossi, M. *Erminia sul Giordano* (Rome, 1637).

Rousseau, J.J. *Dictionnaire de Musique* (Paris, 1767).

Sabbatini, G. *Regola facile e bene per sonare sopra il basso continuo nell'organo, manacordo, o altro simile stromento* (Venice, 1628).

Sangiovanni, G. *Primi ammaestramenti della musica figurata … come pure vi si danno le regole del basso continuo per ben accompagnare nel clavicembalo, et organo la parte che canta e che suona* (Modena, 1714).

Scarlatti, A. *Lezzioni, toccate d'intavolatura per sonare il cembalo. Riproduzione del manoscritto della biblioteca Estense di Modena, introduzione di Luigi Ferdinando Tagliavini.* Facsimile reprint (Bologna, 1999).

Solerti, A. *Le origini del melodramma* (Turin, 1903). Facsimile reprint (Bologna, 1983).

Spencer, R. in 'Letters', comments on 'Florentine Continuo c. 1600', *Early Music*, vol. 11 (1983), p. 575.

Storace, B. *Selva di varie composizioni d'intavolatura per cimbalo ed organo* (Venice, 1664). Facsimile reprint (Florence, 1982).

Strozzi, G. *Capricci da sonare cembali, et organi* (Naples, 1687). Facsimile reprint (Florence, 1979).

Tagliavini, L.F. 'L'armonico pratico al cimbalo – Lettura critica', *Quaderni della Rivista Italiana di musicologia 6*, ed. F. della Seta and F. Piperno (Florence, 1981), pp. 133–55.

Tagliavini, L.F. 'L'arte di "non lasciar vuoto lo strumento": appunti sulla prassi cembalistica italiana nel Cinque- e Seicento', *Rivista Italiana di musicologia*, vol. 10 (1975), pp. 360–78.

Tagliavini, L.F. et al., 'Problemi di prassi esecutiva', *Quaderni della Rivista Italiana di musicologia 3*, ed. A. Cavicchi, O. Mischiati and P. Petrobelli (Florence, 1972), pp. 111–25.

Tagliavini, L.F. 'Review of Helmut Haack, Anfänge des Generalbaßsatzes. Die "Cento Concerti Ecclesiastici" (1602) von Lodovico Viadana (Tutzing, Hans Schneider 1974')', *Rivista Italiana di Musicologia*, 13, (1978), pp. 174–85.

Tomeoni, P. *Regole pratiche per accompagnare il basso continuo* (Florence, 1795).

Toni, A. 'Sul basso continuo e l'interpretazione della Musica antica', *Rivista musicale Italiana*, vol. 26 (1918), pp. 229–64.

Torchi, L. 'L'accompagnamento degl'istrumenti nei melodrammi italiani della prima metà del seicento', *Rivista musicale Italiana*, vol. 1 (1894), pp. 7–38.

Turini, F. *Madrigali à cinque cioè tre voci, e due violini con un basso continuo duplicato per un chitarrone o simil istromento* (Venice, 1629).

Veracini, F.M. *Sonate accademiche a violino solo e basso, Opera seconda* (London and Florence, 1744). Facsimile reprint (Florence, 1990).

Viadana, L. *Cento concerti ecclesiastici a una, a due, a tre, e quattro voci. Con il basso continuo per sonar nell'organo* (Venice, 1602).

Williams, P. *The European Organ 1450–1850* (London, 1966).

Zacconi, L. *Prattica di musica* (Venice, 1596). Facsimile reprint (Bologna, 1983).

Manuscripts

Bologna, Museo internazionale e biblioteca della musica di Bologna

E. 25, *Regole di canto figurato, contrapunto, d'accompagnare.*

K. 22, *Modo pratico per accompagnare sul cembalo, od organo.*

K. 36, *Regole per sonar il basso continuo del sig. del P. Giuseppe Natali da Camerino, Regole di Baglioni.*

K. 81, *Regole per li principianti da suonare il basso sopra il clavicembalo, o spinetta.*

P. 120, *Compendio d'alcune regole principali che compongono il musical contrapunto; Auertimenti per accompagnar la parte con regole generali; Regole del contrapunto, per sonare il basso continuo, et accompagnare la parte che canta; 'Le consonanze sono 5 cioè unison 8 5 3 6'; Regole d'accompagnamento; Regole del basso continuo, cioè per sapere sonare il cembalo ò spinetta ridotte in questa forma, e copiate in questo modo per più commodità, del sig. r Alessandro Stradella.*

P. 132, *Regole per imparare à sonare il cimbalo, ò organo*, 1714.

P. 134, *Regole del contrapunto; Regole per sonare sopra la parte; Regole per accompagnar il basso continuo; Regole del sonare; Regola del contrappunto di Lorenzo Penna; Regole per il basso; Vera regola e modo d'imparare di suonare sopra la parte; Canoni all'unisono; Intonazioni di canto fermo col basso per accompagnarle con alcune regole per accompagnare il canto fermo.*

P. 138, *Regola di canto figurato, e contrapunto, et ancora il vero modo di sonare sopra la parte*, 1684; *Regula di sonare sopra la parte*, 1663; *Regole per l'accompagnatura del basso continuo; Istrutioni per intendere il contrapunto et il modo ancora di saper suonar con tutte le regole nella tastatura il basso continuo*, 1699.

P. 140, *Esercitio per imparare di sonar sopra la parte; Regole generali per saper accompagnare; Regole del sonare il basso continuo* [Pannuzzo Pannuzzi]; *Regole per sonare il cembalo sopra la parte del basso continuo; Regole per sonare sù la Parte d'autore ignoto.*

Durante, F. *Partimenti, ossia intero studio di numerati per ben suonare il cembalo*, EE. 171.

Pannuzzi, P. *see* P. 140.

Pasquini, B. *Regole del Sig. Bernardo Pasquini per bene accompagnare con il cembalo, ad uso di Giuseppe Gaetani da Tofi. In Roma dal dì 7 gennaio 1715*, D. 138.

Stradella, A. *see* P. 120.

Tonelli, A. *Teorica musicale ordinata alla moderna pratica*, L. 54.

London, The British Library

Scarlatti, A. *Per accompagnare il cembalo, ò organo, ò altro stromento*, MS Add. 14244, pp. 39–52.

Milan, Biblioteca del Conservatorio 'Giuseppe Verdi'

Greco, G. *Partimenti, ossiano studj di contrappunto, originali del Maestro Greco Gaetano*, MS Noseda Z 16-13.

Modena, Biblioteca Estense Universitaria

Tonelli, A. *Della quint'opra d'Arcangiol Corelli* / *Basso per tasto d'Antonio Tonelli*, Mus. F 1174.

Naples, Biblioteca del Conservatorio di Musica 'S. Pietro a Majella'

Gasparini, F. *Cantata, Andate ò miei sospiri*, MS 6.3.5.
Paisiello, G. *Regole per bene accompagnare il partimento, o sia il basso fondamentale*, MS 33-2-3.
Scarlatti, A. *Da sventura à sventura*, MS 34.5.2.
Scarlatti, A. *Primo e secondo libro di Toccate del Sig. Cavagliere Alessandro Scarlatti*, MS 34.6.31. Facsimile reprint (Florence, 1981).

Rome, Biblioteca dell'Accademia Nazionale dei Lincei e Corsiniana

MS Musica R. 1, *Regole accompagnar sopra la parte N.1 d'autore incerto.*
Musica P. 15, *Regole più necessarie, e universali per accompagnare il basso continuo con l'arcileuto, ò gravicembalo.*

Rome, Biblioteca Apostolica Vaticana

MS Chigi, Q. IV. 28.

Venice, Biblioteca Nazionale Marciana

Ziani, M.A. *Serenata La Flora*, cl. 4, n.572, 9852.

Index of Subjects

Index of Proper Names